NO LONGER THE PROPERTY OF
BALDWIN PUBLIC LIBRARY

SADDAM HUSSEIN

SADDAM

BY REBECCA STEFOFF

HUSSEIN

THE MILLBROOK PRESS, INC.
BROOKFIELD, CONNECTICUT

BALDWIN PUBLIC LIBRARY

Photographs courtesy of Sipa Press: pp. 13 (Jorge Ferrari),
18 (Collection Francoise Demulder), 23 (both, Fouad Matar),
27 (Jose Nicolas), 39 (Faoud Matar), 52 (Adnan), 61 (Faoud
Matar), 79 (Alfred), 97; AP/Wide World: pp. 44, 62, 85, 99;
UPI/Bettmann: pp. 69, 82; Reuters/Bettmann: pp. 94, 103, 106.
Map by Frank Senyk.

Library of Congress Cataloging-in-Publication Data
Stefoff, Rebecca, 1951–
Saddam Hussein : absolute ruler of Iraq / by Rebecca Stefoff.
          p.   cm.
Includes bibliographical references and index.
Summary: Interweaves the story of Saddam with
that of the nation he rules with an iron hand.
ISBN 1-56294-475-4 (lib. bdg.)
1. Hussein, Saddam, 1937–   —Juvenile literature.   2. Presidents
—Iraq—Biography—Juvenile literature.   I. Title.
DS79.66.H87S74   1995
956.704′4′092—dc20   94-16982   CIP   AC

Published by The Millbrook Press, Inc.
2 Old New Milford Road
Brookfield, Connecticut 06804

Copyright © 1995 by Rebecca Stefoff
Printed in the United States of America
All rights reserved
1   3   5   6   4   2

A NOTE ON SPELLINGS: Arabic names are transliterated into English in a variety of ways, and the same name is often spelled differently in different sources. I wanted to avoid spellings that use diacritics such as the *ayn* and the *hamza* that may be unfamiliar and confusing to readers. Thus for place-names I have followed *Webster's Geographical Dictionary*. For the spelling of proper names I have followed *The New York Times* style.

In the usage of Saddam Hussein's name, I have followed the style of most newspapers, the major newsmagazines, and the majority of scholarly books: I have used the name "Saddam Hussein" in some places, but when using only one name I have favored "Saddam," which is what readers are accustomed to seeing and hearing in the news media. I have, however, referred to him as "Hussein" (the usage favored by encyclopedias) in some places, so that readers should be prepared to encounter all three versions.

CONTENTS

SADDAM HUSSEIN

OVERNIGHT INVASION

THE DESERTS of the Middle East are usually quiet at night. In the cold hours before the sun rises to scorch the sand and rock, the silence is broken only by the occasional call of a night bird or the bark of a fox. But in the hours before dawn on August 2, 1990, the silence along the southern border of Iraq was suddenly shattered. Thousands of engines roared into life. Tanks and trucks lurched into motion, carrying 30,000 Iraqi soldiers across the desert. Behind them, thousands more prepared to move out in their turn. While half the world slept, Iraq's army advanced on the small neighboring nation of Kuwait—a nation that had been one of Iraq's most generous allies.

At about two o'clock in the morning, the vanguard of the invading force stormed across the border into Kuwait. The invaders met little resistance as they headed toward Kuwait City, the capital, 80 miles (130 kilometers) from the border. Arriving on the outskirts of Kuwait City, the Iraqis launched a strong attack.

Sleeping Kuwaitis wakened to the thud of artillery shells exploding and the rattle of machine guns and rifles. Stunned, they looked out their windows to see Iraqi helicopters and jets firing on their city. The sky burst into flame as rockets landed on military bases and other targets around the city.

One of these targets was the Dasman Palace, home of the royal family of Kuwait. Iraqi troops and tanks advanced on the palace, hoping to capture the emir, the country's ruler. But the emir, Jabir al-Ahmad al-Sabah, and most of his family and staff, following a well-rehearsed emergency plan, ran to a convoy of armored cars as soon as they realized that the capital was doomed to fall into Iraqi hands. The emir escaped from the Iraqis—by just six minutes, according to some accounts—and headed straight for Saudi Arabia. His brother Fahd was killed defending the Dasman Palace, and several other members of his family were captured. Most of the emir's relatives managed to flee the country, however. More than a thousand members of the large Sabah clan, the extended family group that includes the emir's distant cousins as well as his immediate family, reached sanctuary with their Saudi allies.

Many of the fleeing officials managed to take at least some of their wealth with them, in the form of jewels and other property. A number of them also made last-minute calls to their banks to have their fortunes transferred out of Kuwait. Yet considerable wealth remained to be seized by the invaders, for Kuwait was an oil-rich nation. In the early hours of the invasion, Iraqi tanks rumbled up to the doors of Kuwait's central bank, where much of the country's cash and gold were stored. Later, Kuwaiti homes and businesses were stripped by the Iraqis in an orgy of looting.

August 2, 1990: Iraqi tanks and armored vehicles take up positions in Kuwait City. After an easily won victory, President Saddam Hussein claimed the small, oil-rich territory for Iraq.

The first wave of Iraqi invaders also targeted the Ministry of Information, a large building that housed Kuwait's state-owned radio and television stations. Terrified Kuwaitis inside the ministry tried desperately to broadcast their plight to the world as gun-wielding members of Iraq's Republican Guard overran the building. One radio announcer cried, "Hurry to our aid—" before the transmission was cut off.

The Kuwaiti armed forces were overwhelmed by the size and speed of the invasion. Kuwait had an army of 16,000, but the first wave alone of the invading force was nearly twice that size. The country's navy consisted of fewer than twenty small vessels and was designed to patrol the offshore waters against smugglers, not to engage in military combat. Only the Kuwaiti air force managed to put up some resistance to the invasion. Kuwaiti pilots destroyed an airfield north of Kuwait City so that Iraqi planes could not land on it, and then they made two bombing runs against the Iraqis. By that time, however, their airfields had been overrun by Iraqi ground troops, making it impossible for them to refuel and reload, so they flew to safety in Saudi Arabia. Ultimately, the strongest resistance to the invasion came in the streets of Kuwait City, where hand-to-hand fighting broke out amid the rubble of bombed buildings. A number of Kuwaitis gallantly attempted to defend their capital, only to be gunned down by the more numerous and better-equipped Iraqis.

Three hours after the first Iraqi troops had crossed the border, Kuwait City was a conquered capital. Despite scattered pockets of resistance, the city was firmly in Iraqi hands. Nonetheless, fresh waves of Iraqi troops and tanks were entering Kuwait. The first wave had consisted of the soldiers of the Republican Guard, Iraq's elite fighting force. The second wave was called the Popular Army, a large but poorly trained and equipped mass of peasants. The third wave consisted of Iraq's regular army troops. These brought the total number of Iraqis in Kuwait to more than 100,000 by the afternoon of August 2. Once the fighting was over, another group of Iraqis arrived in Kuwait City: officers and troops of the Mukhabarat, Iraq's dreaded secret police. They were in charge of rounding up and disposing of any Kuwaitis who openly opposed Iraqi rule.

That day and for many days thereafter, the mastermind behind the swift and shocking invasion dominated newspaper headlines and television news broadcasts around the world. He was Saddam Hussein, president of Iraq, who ruled his country with the powers of a dictator. Now, it seemed, he intended to rule Kuwait as well.

★ ★ ★

THE INVASION caught the world by surprise. Although Saddam Hussein had been massing troops in the border region for many weeks, neither the Kuwaitis nor the Saudis, his neighbors to the south, believed that he would attack. They thought that he was bluffing, using the threat of force to pressure Kuwait into sharing its wealth. Even some Kuwaiti government officials who had feared that Saddam might be planning to attack did not consider the possibility that he would invade the capital and occupy the entire country. At most, they thought, he would seize some territory along the Iraq-Kuwait border, territory that had been disputed between the two countries for years. Other Arab leaders in the Middle East agreed that there was no real danger. Less than two weeks before the invasion, President Hosni Mubarak of Egypt announced that Saddam Hussein had promised him that he was ready to discuss the border dispute.

The United States was caught off guard, too. Although one or two observers in the U.S. Central Intelligence Agency (CIA) warned that the danger to Kuwait was real, the official opinion of the CIA and other government agencies was that Hussein's threats were mere bluster. On July 25, Saddam summoned the U.S. ambassador in Iraq, April Glaspie, to his palace for a meeting. Although he ranted angrily against Kuwait, Glaspie left the meeting convinced that he would not launch an attack. At the very worst, she thought, he would seize a small portion of the disputed border territory. She later told *The New York Times*: "I didn't think—and nobody else did—that the Iraqis were going to take all of Kuwait." Not until the Iraqi troops were just a few hours from crossing the border into Kuwait did the CIA notify President George Bush that an invasion of Kuwait by Iraq was "probable."

In the days and weeks that followed the overnight invasion of Kuwait, world leaders found themselves in a tense stand off with Saddam Hussein. The invasion of one Arab nation by another was painful to the other Arab countries of the region, for it struck a blow against Arab unity. The United States and other Western countries worried that oil prices would go up now that Hussein controlled Kuwait's oilfields, which contain about 10 percent of the world's known oil reserves (Iraq contains 5 percent). Worse yet was the threat that Iraq might invade Saudi Arabia, where the world's largest oilfields—25 percent of all known reserves—are located. If Iraq seized Saudi Arabia, Saddam Hussein would control 40 percent of the world's oil.

The United Nations condemned Saddam's aggression and demanded that Iraqi troops withdraw from Kuwait. But the situation remained a stalemate. Saddam did not back down. Instead, he set up a puppet government in Kuwait City. From Baghdad, the capital of Iraq, he proclaimed that Kuwait was now an Iraqi province.

While heads of state discussed how best to respond to the occupation of Kuwait, the world gazed in horrified fascination upon Saddam Hussein. Almost overnight he had burst upon the public—especially the American public—as a new international villain. His heavy-jowled face, with its dark eyebrows and thick mustache, became instantly recognizable from news reports and political cartoons. Some called him the "Butcher of Baghdad." This gruesome nickname was supported by the stories that began to reach the world from refugees fleeing occupied Kuwait. The refugees told of atrocities committed by Iraqis against Kuwaitis, presumably with Saddam's blessing. The invaders did not just loot and vandalize Iraqi homes. They also raped girls and women. They stole medical supplies and arrested doctors, leaving hospital patients to die in their beds. They arrested thousands of Kuwaitis, many of whom were beaten or tortured. Some were killed. One refugee, a Kuwaiti doctor, told a *New York Times* reporter about such a murder. "They took my best friend, Bedar," the man said, "and the next day they dropped his body in the street. They had wrapped his head in a Kuwaiti flag and fired three bullets into his skull."[1] Another refugee, displaying scores of dark bruises on his back and arms, reported that he had been beaten

Saddam Hussein shares a New
Year's Eve meal with Iraqi
soldiers stationed at
an undisclosed location in
occupied Kuwait.

and tortured with electric shocks because Iraqi soldiers found a picture of the emir of Kuwait in his car.

Stories about Saddam Hussein's background also emerged. He was said to be a master of torture and deceit. He had risen to power by violence, killing all those who seemed to stand in his way, even members of his own family. He had waged a relentless war against the Kurds, an ethnic minority in Iraq, and had used poison gas against his own people. He was known to be desperately eager to develop nuclear power so that he could arm Iraq with nuclear weapons. Most disturbing to many Americans was the fact that the United States had provided Saddam with a great deal of money and technology, hoping to make him an ally. Now he was using those resources to start a war in the Persian Gulf—a war that might involve the United States.

Saddam's character was endlessly analyzed. To many, he was merely a dangerous, powerful madman. One Saudi prince said, "We always thought he was possessed of a pure criminal mentality, but now he is going crazy."[2] Some Israeli defense officials agreed that Saddam suffered from a form of mental illness. American president George Bush regarded him as a second Adolf Hitler, evil and deranged. Yet others who had studied Saddam's career pointed out that he could also be viewed as a shrewd, cynical, and survival-oriented manipulator.

As the Kuwait crisis continued, most Americans realized that they knew little or nothing about the man who had ruled Iraq for more than a decade and now occupied the center of the world stage. Nor did they know very much about the history of Iraq and Kuwait, or about the troubled state of affairs in Iraq that had allowed Saddam Hussein to rise to power.

THE BIRTHPLACE OF HISTORY

SADDAM HUSSEIN was born on April 28, 1937, in the village of al-Auja, a cluster of mud huts on the outskirts of the town of Tikrit in northern Iraq. Tikrit, located on the banks of the Tigris River, is a thousand years old. It has figured largely in several episodes of Iraq's history. Tikrit was the birthplace of Saladin, a Muslim warrior hero who battled the Christian Crusaders in the twelfth century. In the fourteenth century, it was a center of resistance against the Mongol hordes who swept across Iraq from Central Asia. By the nineteenth century, however, the town's importance had dwindled. Visitors to Tikrit remarked that the only subjects of interest were the crumbling ruins of a castle and the skill of the local craftsmen at making *kalaks,* round rafts of inflated animal skins.

Saddam was proud that he came from Tikrit, even though Tikrit was nothing more than a humble up-country town when he was born. The railway from Baghdad to Mosul, the principal city of northern Iraq, ran through Tikrit, but the town had only one road. It had no electricity or piped water; people burned cow dung for fuel and drew water from ancient wells.

Saddam's childhood was one of poverty and humiliation. His father, a landless peasant named Hussein al-Majid al-Tikriti, disappeared either shortly before or soon after Saddam's birth. The official account of Saddam's life claims that his father was killed by bandits, but an Iraqi who formerly worked as the president's secretary says that Hussein simply deserted his pregnant wife Subha. Saddam was born in the house of Khayrallah Tulfah, his mother's brother. But it was his father's brother who gave the newborn boy his name, which means "the clasher" or "the one who confronts."

Subha was unable to support her infant son, so she left him in the care of his uncle Khayrallah Tulfah for the first few years of his life. Khayrallah was an educated man, an army officer, and a person of some distinction in Tikrit. Unfortunately for Saddam, however, in 1941 Khayrallah was sentenced to five years in jail for taking part in a military uprising. Young Saddam had to leave the relative comfort of his uncle's home to live with his mother in the tiny village of al-Shawish, not far from Tikrit.

Subha had remarried, and Saddam discovered that his stepfather, Ibrahim Hassan, was vicious and illiterate. Ibrahim beat and insulted the boy, refusing to let him go to school. "He is a son of a dog," Ibrahim would shout to Subha. "Give him away, I don't want him."[1] Ibrahim often thrashed Saddam with a stick covered with asphalt. In later years Saddam recalled with anger how his stepfather would yank him from bed before dawn and shove him outside to tend the family sheep. Ibrahim also made young Saddam steal chickens and sheep, which he then sold. As a result of this and other activities, the Ibrahim family were regarded by their neighbors as thugs and thieves. Saddam was a social outcast. The village boys tormented him, mocking him for not having a father, until he began carrying a heavy iron bar with which to defend himself.

This dismal existence ended when Saddam was ten years old. His uncle Khayrallah Tulfah had been released from jail and had returned to Tikrit. One day Saddam appeared at his uncle's house, saying that he wished to stay there. According to one version of the story, the only possession the boy carried with him was a pistol he had somehow obtained. It is not known whether Saddam ran away from home or whether his stepfather sent him away, but in either case Saddam's mother would have had little to say in the matter, for as a woman in an Islamic country she was expected to submit to the decisions made by the men of her family.

When he joined his uncle's household, Saddam's life changed. Khayrallah enrolled Saddam in the same primary school attended by his own son, Adnan Khayrallah, who was three years younger than Saddam. The two boys got along well, and Adnan Khayrallah became Saddam's closest friend. Education, however, did not come easily to Saddam. Back in al-Shawish he had yearned to go to school, but now he was embarrassed to be so far behind the other boys. At the age of ten he could not even write his name. To cover his shame, he became a clown, trying to amuse his schoolmates with practical jokes and cruel pranks—for example, while pretending to give an elderly teacher a friendly hug, he would put a snake inside the man's robe. But with the help and encouragement of his un-

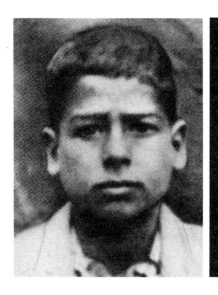

A rare photo of Saddam as a boy in the 1940s, from a biography by Faoud Matar. His childhood was filled with poverty, violence, and rejection.

Saddam's mother, Subha. Saddam's father disappeared before his birth. He was either killed or, more likely, abandoned his family. (Photo from the Matar biography.)

cle, he learned to read and write. He graduated from intermediate school (equivalent to junior high) at the age of sixteen.

By this time, Khayrallah Tulfah had left Tikrit for Baghdad, where he became a schoolteacher. After his graduation from school in Tikrit, Saddam followed his beloved uncle to the capital, about 100 miles (160 kilometers) south of Tikrit. This was Saddam's first venture away from his home district. Baghdad offered the teenage Saddam an exciting glimpse of life beyond the mud villages and drowsy small towns of rural northern Iraq. The Baghdad of the 1950s was a busy, cosmopolitan city, a hotbed of political activity. This lively capital was Saddam Hussein's introduction to the larger world of history and politics—a world that he entered at a particularly turbulent time in the history of Iraq.

★ ★ ★

IRAQ'S HISTORY, as Saddam Hussein would never tire of reminding his subjects, was a glorious one. Indeed, one of Saddam's strategies for strengthening his hold on the people of Iraq was to tell them that his rule was a return to the glories of the country's golden past. He did not hesitate to compare himself to the kings and heroes of ancient empires.

Iraq is regarded by many historians as the birthplace of Western history. Some of the oldest known human settlements, dating from 10,000 B.C., have been found in a region that is now the heart of Iraq. This region, bounded by the Tigris and Euphrates rivers, was called Mesopotamia. It was the cradle of many ancient civilizations.

The Sumerians, whose civilization reached its height about 3200 B.C., built large city-states and de-

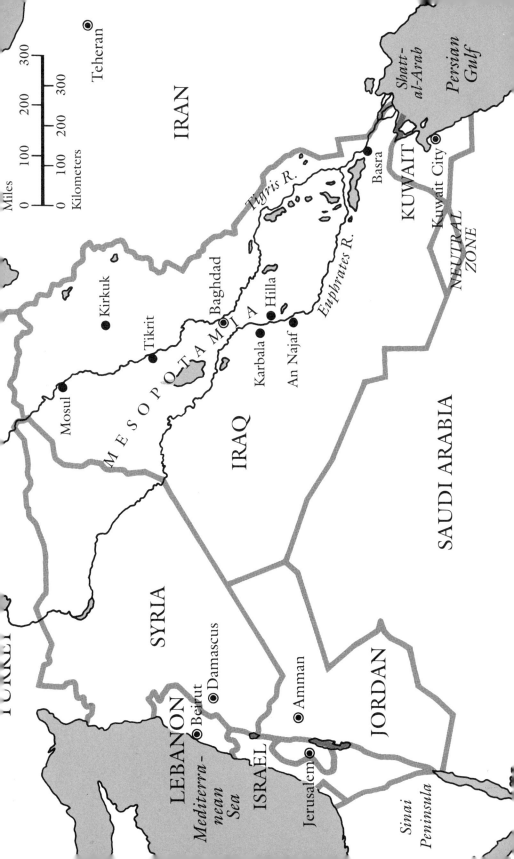

veloped a written language—the beginning of recorded history. They were succeeded by the Akkadians, who built the city of Babylon on a branch of the Euphrates, near the site of the present-day town of Hilla. The most noteworthy ruler of early Babylon was Hammurabi, who created the first formal code of laws in the eighteenth century B.C. About 1000 B.C. a people called the Assyrians overcame Babylon and founded their own empire. The Assyrians cultivated a reputation for fierceness and cruelty, hoping that other peoples would fear them and thus be easy to dominate—a strategy that Saddam Hussein was to adopt many centuries later.

Assyrian power declined in the seventh century B.C., and Babylonian civilization revived. In the sixth century, Babylon was rebuilt by Nebuchadnezzar, who appears in the Bible as the king who conquered Jerusalem and led its Hebrew inhabitants into captivity in Babylon: an ancient example of the strife that still exists between the modern states of Israel and Iraq. Nebuchadnezzar's Babylon was magnificent, full of towers and temples. Its "hanging gardens"—probably trees and vines planted on terraces high above street level—were one of the fabled wonders of the ancient world.

About 539 B.C., Mesopotamia was conquered by invaders from Persia, its neighbor to the east. This was the first of many clashes between the countries today known as Iraq and Iran. Except for a few periods of Greek or Roman rule, Mesopotamia was ruled by Persia for hundreds of years.

In the seventh century A.D., a sudden new force swept out of the deserts of Arabia to change the face of the world. That force was Islam, a faith founded by the Arab prophet Muhammad. By the time of Muham-

A scene in reconstructed Babylon, an ancient trading and religious center on the banks of the Euphrates near present-day Baghdad. The first record of this city dates from 2200 B.C.

mad's death in 632, Islam was firmly established in central Arabia. A few years later, Arab Muslims, as followers of Islam are called, had begun a process of expansion and conquest that would carry their faith, their language, and their culture far beyond the Arabian Peninsula. The Muslim empire would eventually include North Africa, most of the Middle East, and parts of Spain and South Asia.

Mesopotamia was one of the first places to be swept by Islam. By 642 the Arabs had defeated the Persians and established Arab rule in Mesopotamia, which they renamed Iraq. This conquest transformed the country more profoundly than any of the previous invasions. Before long, Arabs formed the ethnic majority among the population. Iraq had become an Arab land, with Arabic as its primary language and Islam as its faith. (Persia, by contrast, was not extensively occupied by Arabs, although most Persians converted to Islam. Iran, Persia's modern descendant, is an Islamic nation but not an Arab one.)

The early years of the Islamic empire were torn by religious conflict. A dispute arose over who was to follow Muhammad as the next caliph, or head of the Islamic faith. One faction, the Shia, supported Ali, Muhammad's son-in-law; Ali's followers were called the Shiite Muslims. An opposing faction, the Sunni Muslims, supported various figures among the aristocracy of Mecca, the Arabian city that is the holiest site in Islam. Rivalry between the Shiites and Sunnis led to civil war. Much of the fighting took place in Iraq, and two Iraqi towns became holy shrines to the Shiites: Najaf, where Ali was buried, and Karbala, where Ali's son Hussein was killed by a Sunni army.

The legacy of this seventh-century conflict lives on in the Muslim world today. In several Islamic countries, Shiites and Sunnis are pitted against one another, with the stronger party using its power to persecute the weaker. Iran's Muslims are nearly all Shiites. The Shiite version of Islam is the official state religion of Iran, and Sunnis are a mistrusted minority. But in Iraq, although the majority of the people are Shiites, the minority Sunnis have traditionally been more powerful. As a result, the Shiites have suffered frequent persecution at the hands of Iraq's Sunni leaders, including Saddam Hussein. The centuries-old rivalry between Shiites and Sunnis is one element in the ongoing hostility between Iran and Iraq.

Despite the early fighting between Shiites and Sunnis, Islam remained strong. From 750 until 1258, Iraq was the center of an Islamic empire that stretched from Central Asia across North Africa. Its capital was Baghdad, built on the banks of the Tigris in the heart of Mesopotamia. Baghdad was the center not only of political life but also of a great outburst of Islamic culture and learning. While Europe was languishing in the early Middle Ages, Islamic geographers, doctors, mathematicians, and writers launched a Renaissance, drawing on Persian, Greek, and Arabic traditions.

Political life in this period had some important features that were later adopted by Saddam Hussein. First, government officials created a highly structured, centralized bureaucracy that kept a tight grip over every detail of local government; this central government was aided by a vast network of spies and informers. Second, an elaborate set of court rituals and rules governed the way the caliph was treated. For example, only the highest-ranking officials in the empire could speak directly to the caliph, and even they had to bow many times and kiss the ground before they could approach him. This lofty code of conduct turned the caliph into a remote, godlike figure whose every word was law. Such a state of affairs was contrary to the original Islamic tradition, which held that the caliph was one of the people. In the twentieth century, Hussein duplicated these features of the earlier empire: a powerful central government, the use of spies and informers, and the elevation of the ruler into a godlike hero.

In the thirteenth and fourteenth centuries, Mongol warlords overran and looted Iraq, carrying their spoils back to their Central Asian homeland. Iraq sank into chaos and economic depression. The next power to arise in the region was the Ottoman empire, based in Turkey. The Ottoman Turks were Sunni Muslims who wanted to create a new Islamic empire. They gained control of Iraq in the sixteenth century, and Iraq remained in Ottoman hands for nearly 400 years, a period that historian Phebe Marr calls "the centuries of stagnation."[2] During this time, Iraq was a backwater of the Ottoman empire. Yet these centuries were vitally important in shaping the social structure of modern Iraq.

At this time, Iraq did not exist as a single, unified country. Instead, it consisted of three provinces, each centered upon a major city: Basra in the south, near the head of the Persian Gulf; Baghdad in central Mesopotamia; and Mosul in the north, near the Turkish border. The Ottomans ruled the cities, but their power did not extend far into the countryside, where tribal chieftains held sway. Many of the rural people were Arabs who had migrated north from Arabia. Under the influence of the Shiite religious centers at Najaf and

Karbala, they became Shiites, and they were often at odds with the Sunni governors of the cities. No one but the Turkish governors felt any real loyalty to the Ottoman empire, or to the Turkish sultan in his faraway capital of Istanbul. Iraqis identified themselves with their clan, with the community or district where they lived, or with the branch of Islam they followed. This factionalism and tribalism has survived into present-day Iraq. Loyalty to family, clan, or region is much stronger in many Iraqis' lives than the fragile sense of national identity.

★   ★   ★

DURING THE YEARS of Ottoman rule, Europeans began appearing in the Middle East. In the nineteenth century, the British gained a toehold on the coast of the Persian Gulf, close to Basra. A rebellious clan there called the Sabahs had won independence from the Ottomans in the early eighteenth century. The Sabahs' territory came to be known as Kuwait. Britain made a treaty with the emir of Kuwait in 1899. In exchange for a cash payment and the promise of British protection against the Ottomans, the emir agreed not to let Britain's European rivals, such as Germany and Russia, trade in Kuwait.

Ottoman rule of Iraq ended during World War I. When the war broke out in 1914, the Ottoman empire sided with Germany and Austria-Hungary, and thus came under attack from Britain and France. British forces entered the Middle East to wage war against the Turks in the desert. The British seized Basra first, and by the end of the war they controlled all of Iraq. In the meantime, Britain and France had made a secret deal to divide the Ottoman territories between them when the war ended. Under this agreement, Iraq and Palestine would come under British influence, and Syria and Lebanon would go to France.

The end of the war brought not only the collapse of the Ottoman empire but also a wave of energy and optimism throughout the Middle East. Many Arabs hoped for independence. They had been ruled by the Ottomans for 400 years. Now, with the Ottomans gone, they wanted to take control of their own destinies. But Britain and France, the European powers who emerged victorious from the war, did not share this view. They wanted to retain economic and political control of the Middle East, and they argued that the countries, sheikhdoms, and provinces of the regions, demoralized and bankrupt after centuries of foreign domination, were not ready for independence. The League of Nations, the forerunner of today's United Nations, agreed. It gave Britain and France mandates over various parts of the region. Under these mandates, the European countries were supposed to establish new governments in the liberated Arab lands and prepare them for eventual self-rule.

Britain's mandate included Iraq, which Britain created as a new nation in 1920 by joining together the three former Ottoman provinces of Mosul, Baghdad, and Basra. But the British drew Iraq's borders with little regard for how they would affect the people of the new country. In the north, for example, the border with Turkey followed the old Ottoman provincial border, even though this border ran through the middle of the mountainous homeland of the Kurds, a non-Arab Islamic people who had been promised a nation of their own by the British. The British did not keep their promise, and the hoped-for state of Kurdistan was divided among Turkey, Iraq, Iran, and Russia, leading to decades of conflict. Since 1920, the Kurds of Iraq have frequently rebelled against the Iraqi government. They have also been the victims of ethnic prejudice and persecution. Although Kurds make up 20 percent of the population of Iraq—they are the nation's largest non-Arab minority—they remain second-class citizens within their country.

The British created another border problem on Iraq's southern coast. When the Kuwaitis grew angry because the British had given part of their territory to Saudi Arabia, Britain made amends by giving a stretch of Iraq's coastline to Kuwait. This reduced Iraq to a mere 16 miles (26 kilometers) of marshy coastline, without a single good harbor—another cause of long-lived border disputes.

The Iraqis, newly liberated from Ottoman rule, were by no means eager to submit to the British. As soon as the British mandate was announced, riots and revolts sprang up throughout the land. "Arab rule for Arabs!" the Iraqis demanded. The British responded to this demand by giving them an Arab king. They set up a monarchy and chose Faisal, a Sunni Muslim and a son of the sheikh of Mecca, to be the first king of Iraq. Faisal took the throne in 1921. The early years of his rule were plagued by strife and disunion as he tried to set up modern government institutions. Faisal often brooded about the lack of national identity among the people he had been sent to govern. He wrote, "I say with my heart full of sadness that there is not yet in Iraq an Iraqi people."[3]

The people of Iraq were united in one thing, however: Nearly all of them wanted the British overlordship of their country to end. Because of their unceasing demands for independence, Iraq was the first Arab state to shed its status as a mandated territory. Britain's mandate ended in 1932, and Iraq became independent. That same year, Iraq entered the League of Nations, the first Arab country to do so. But even then Iraq's independence was not complete. In order to be released from the mandate, Iraq had to sign a treaty that gave Britain certain privileges, including the right to keep military bases in Iraq. On top of their general resentment of European domination, many Iraqis were especially indignant that their freedom to govern themselves was linked with these concessions to Britain. The British presence in Iraq was a sore point with a large part of the population. Nationalism, the feeling that Iraq should be completely free of British influence, grew stronger, especially among Iraqi army officers. So did pan-Arabism, the vision of a unified Arab community in North Africa and the Middle East (the prefix *pan* means "all").

King Faisal died in 1933 and was succeeded as king by his son Ghazi. When Ghazi died in 1939, his son, Faisal II, was too young to take the throne. Ghazi's brother Abdul Illah became regent, ruling Iraq in the young prince's name. In that year World War II broke out in Europe, pitting Nazi Germany against Britain and its allies. Some Iraqi nationalists, including Saddam Hussein's uncle, Khayrallah Tulfah, supported the Nazis, hoping that a German victory would cut Britain's lingering hold on Iraq and other Middle Eastern countries.

In the spring of 1941, a group of nationalist officers in the Iraqi army carried out a coup. They forced Abdul Illah, the regent, to flee the country, and they named a leading nationalist, Rashid Ali al-Kailani, as

Iraq's new prime minister. Ali declared war on Britain and ordered the Iraqi army to attack the British air bases in Iraq. British forces quickly subdued the Iraqis, Britain regained its strong influence in Iraq, and the regent was restored to his post. Rashid Ali fled the country. Khayrallah Tulfah, along with other officers who had supported Ali's coup and fought against Britain, was expelled from the army and sent to jail.

World War II ended in 1945, but peace brought a new source of strife to the Middle East. The League of Nations, with the support of Britain, the United States, and other Western powers, decreed that part of Palestine would be given to Jews who had returned to their ancestral homeland. The war had made the need for a Jewish state more pressing. The Jews of Europe had suffered horribly; millions were slaughtered by the Nazis in the Holocaust. Many people throughout the world sympathized with the suffering of the Jews and supported their desire to have a state of their own. But the formation of the Jewish state of Israel in 1948 enraged the Arab states of the region, who felt that the Western nations had no right to dispose of territory that did not belong to them.

In the civil war that erupted between Arabs and Jews in 1947, thousands of Palestinian Arabs fled from Israel to become refugees in other Arab countries. Jews who lived in Arab countries were the target of violence. In Baghdad's ancient Jewish community, nearly 200 Jews were killed in riots from 1947 to 1949; by 1949, the majority of Iraq's Jewish population had left the country. Although Israel brought new hope and national pride to Jews around the world, it also created another division in the Arab world and gave the Arabs another reason to resent the West.

★ ★ ★

THIS WAS the situation in Iraq when young Saddam Hussein arrived in Baghdad in 1953. The rulers of Iraq were friendly toward Britain and the West, but anti-Western feeling was strong among the army and the peasants. Various factions struggled for power; unrest swept the country like a wind. Saddam sensed large events looming on the horizon. Iraq was on the verge of change, and he wanted to be part of it.

COMING-OF-AGE IN BAGHDAD

UPON ARRIVING in Baghdad, Saddam settled into his uncle's house in Karkh, a neighborhood on the west bank of the Tigris where many people from Tikrit lived. Surrounded by relatives and family associates, he found it easy to remember his identity as a Tikriti. His strongest bonds were to his uncle and his fellow Tikritis; later, when he came to power, he would fill most of the high offices in the land with clan members from Tikrit.

Saddam had always admired photographs of his uncle in his soldier's uniform. He hoped to follow in Khayrallah Tulfah's footsteps and become an army officer. But his grades were too poor for admission to the Baghdad Military Academy, the gateway to officer training. To his intense disappointment, Saddam was turned down; his hopes for a military career were shattered. This frustration rankled within him for years.

In the meantime, he enrolled in high school, where he took pains to impress his fellow students by his skill with firearms. According to an official biography authorized by Saddam, he was fascinated with guns from the age of ten and seldom went anywhere without one. By the time he entered high school, he may already have committed his first murder: Some sources say that at the age of sixteen he helped Khayrallah Tulfah kill a man in Tikrit, although details are murky. Another killing is said to have taken place when Saddam was twenty. He and Khayrallah boasted that they had killed a civil servant over political differences. They were caught and put in jail, but they were soon set free for lack of evidence against them. Throughout his career, from high school all the way to the presidency, Saddam encouraged the spread of rumors about these and other violent incidents. According to Efraim Karsh and Inauri Ratsi, authors of *Saddam Hussein: A Political Biography*, Saddam believed that such stories made up for his lack of military experience—and they also made people fear him, which was precisely the reaction he wanted.[1]

The strongest influence on Saddam's beliefs and values was Khayrallah Tulfah, whom he regarded as a foster father. Khayrallah was not a benevolent man. Like many Arabs, he felt a bitter resentment against Britain and the Western powers who had carved up the Arab world after World War I and dominated it for decades. Khayrallah's anti-imperialist feelings deepened after the British crushed the coup in which he participated and sent him to jail. But the British were not the only targets of his hatred. He despised all non-Arabs, and he even loathed Arabs who did not share his political views.

The prejudices that Khayrallah Tulfah passed on to Saddam Hussein can be seen in a little book Khayrallah wrote. It is called *Three Whom God Should Not Have*

Khayrallah Tulfah, Saddam's
maternal uncle, who took the place
of his absent father. (Photo from
the Matar biography.)

Created: Persians, Jews, and Flies. In this pamphlet, which Saddam arranged to have printed and distributed after he became president, Khayrallah explains God's mistakes. Persians or Iranians are, he claims, "animals God created in the shape of humans." Jews are "a mixture of dirt and leftovers of diverse peoples." Flies, in comparison, are only a nuisance "whom we do not understand God's purpose in creating."[2]

Khayrallah's greed and cruelty earned him many enemies. In 1981, when a landowner threatened to sue Khayrallah for illegally seizing his property, Khayrallah replied with a shrug, "Why waste your time? If we are in power, you will get nothing and you will only hurt yourself. If we are overthrown, you won't get one centimeter of my flesh because there are so many people waiting to cut me up."[3]

Under the guidance of this uncle, the young Saddam Hussein became interested in politics. He acquired a growing awareness of Iraq's place in the Arab world and of events outside Iraq. The 1950s were a time of ferment throughout the Middle East. In Egypt an army officer named Gamal Abdel Nasser led a coup in 1952 to overthrow the monarchy that had been sponsored by Britain. Nasser became a hero to Arab nationalists—that is, to those who wanted to eliminate Western domination from their countries.

Nasser's admirers cheered again in 1955, when Nasser defied the United States by buying weapons from the Soviet Union, the Americans' chief enemy in world affairs. A few months later, Nasser went even further and nationalized the Suez Canal, declaring it to be Egyptian property and under the sole control of Egypt. (The canal, which ran through a corner of Egypt and provided a shortcut for shipping between the Mediterranean and Red seas, had been built by France and administered by the European powers.) Britain and France responded to the nationalization of the canal by attacking Egypt, but in the end Egypt kept the canal, and Nasser's popularity soared in the Arab world. In Iraq, people grew increasingly discontented with their king, Faisal II, who had taken the throne in 1953 at the age of eighteen, and with Nuri Said, his prime minister. Many Iraqis thought that the monarchy was a tool of the West, out of step with the mood of Arab nationalism that was running through the land.

Anti-government riots broke out across Iraq in the fall of 1956. The streets of Baghdad filled with angry mobs as students, peasants, and political dissidents called for the end of the monarchy. Saddam roamed the streets, undisturbed by the violent atmosphere. It was probably at this time that he left high school. Various sources claim that he was expelled because of either political or criminal activities. No details are known, but it is certain that he did not graduate from the Karkh high school. Expulsion did not upset Saddam, however, for he had found a new role as a political agitator and conspirator.

Through his uncle, Saddam became part of an Arab political movement called the Baath party (*baath* means "rebirth" or "renaissance" in Arabic). Baathism arose in Syria in the early 1940s. It was founded by two Syrian Arabs, one Christian and one Muslim. The Christian founder of Baath, Michel Aflaq, later moved to Iraq and was associated with Saddam Hussein's regime until his death in 1989.

Unlike some movements that have swept the Arab world in recent decades, Baathism is secular—that is, it is not a religious movement. It does not call for a rebirth of Islamic fervor. Instead, Baathism was built on purely political goals. The Baathists wanted to spread the revolutionary spirit among the Arab countries until all "traces of colonialism," as Aflaq said, had been wiped out. They wanted to cut all ties with the Western nations and to take full control of their own resources and destinies. The Baathists also refused to recognize the national borders that were created by the Europeans at the end of the Ottoman empire. To the Baath party, the entire Arab world from North Africa to Iraq was a single nation, which the Baathists hoped would become a unified Arab state. This pan-Arabism was the strongest element of Baath philosophy. The Baathists felt that all Arabs should stick together. Their ties to one another should outweigh tribal, religious, or regional loyalties. Arab unity should be a more powerful force than Islamic unity—for example, a Muslim Arab should feel more unity with a Christian Arab than with a Muslim Turk or Iranian. "One Arab Nation with an Eternal Mission," was the Baath slogan.

The Baathists wanted to follow Nasser's lead and overthrow the governments that the Western powers had set up in Arab countries. This goal was shared by the growing number of Communists in Syria and Iraq. But the Baathists bitterly opposed the Arab Communists, who were not interested in pan-Arabism but instead wanted to establish ties with the Soviet Union and the Communist nations of Eastern Europe. However, although the Communist movement grew rapidly, the Baath party grew slowly. It had only about 300 members in Iraq by the mid-1950s, and for some time it remained too small and weak to influence events. Nevertheless, Saddam joined the party in 1957, sponsored by his uncle.

The Baathists and the Communists were not the only ones who were dissatisfied with the state of affairs in Iraq. The army had grown larger and more powerful every year since Iraq achieved independence, and among the officer corps were many nationalists who plotted against the monarchy. In 1958 a group of these "Free Officers," as they called themselves, took action. Headed by General Abdul Karim Qassim, they led armed troops into Baghdad and captured the radio station and the palace. The king and his uncle, the former regent, were shot in the palace garden; their bodies were dragged through the streets.

News of the coup was released to the public over the radio. Hundreds of dissidents took to the streets to celebrate the end of the monarchy. Mobs set the British embassy afire and murdered several Jordanians and a Western businessman. Crowds hailed Qassim as a patriot and a hero.

Within a few hours the coup was complete. Qassim declared Iraq a republic with himself at its head. Despite the bloodiness of his coup, Qassim was in some ways a well-meaning ruler. He hoped to end ethnic prejudice and violence against the Shiites and the Kurds; his mother was a Shiite Kurd. Yet he could not risk allowing the Kurds to split off from Iraq to form their own nation, for he feared this would drastically weaken Iraq. When the Kurds realized that Qassim would not grant them independence, they rebelled, and by 1961 a new civil war was raging in the north between Kurdish guerrillas and the Iraqi army.

Some of Qassim's other projects were more successful. Vowing to improve the lives of Iraq's landless peasant masses, he began a policy of land reform, breaking up the huge estates of wealthy landowners. He

July 24, 1958: General Abdul Karim Qassim (left foreground) is surrounded by armed guards as he leaves the captured Baghdad radio station from which he announced to the Iraqi population the overthrow of the monarchy.

spent a quarter of each year's budget on public housing, building thousands of houses for the poor. These actions made Qassim popular with the Iraqi people. Hanna Batatu, author of a history of modern Iraq, says, "The people had more genuine affection for him than for any other ruler in the modern history of Iraq."[4]

Despite his popularity with the masses, Qassim's hold on power was shaky from the start. The Communists soon turned against him because he did not adopt their plans; the pan-Arab nationalists turned against him when he resisted pressure to join an Arab union headed by President Nasser of Egypt. The nationalists and Communists also fought one another, most notably during prolonged rioting in the northern city of Mosul in 1959. Hundreds of people were killed in that outbreak of violence. This climate of unrest bred numerous assassination plots, but Qassim managed to survive the first few attempts on his life. The Baathists grew desperate, fearful of the growing strength of the Communists and the rising tide of violence against nationalists and pan-Arabists. They believed that Qassim had to be removed before Iraq fell apart. In 1959 they tried to assassinate him.

Saddam Hussein so far had not been a particularly distinguished member of the Baath party. His role had been limited to organizing student protests and riots, and to leading a gang of Tikriti thugs who terrorized the Karkh neighborhood, beating up political opponents and non-Tikritis. Now, however, senior Baathists in Baghdad picked him for a more ambitious job. He was part of a six-man team assigned to kill President Qassim.

Three of the young Baathists were supposed to carry out the actual assassination. Two of them had guns; the third had a hand grenade. The other three men were told to hang back and provide covering fire to shield the killers from Qassim's bodyguards. Saddam was assigned to be one of the three secondary shooters. The plan, however, turned out differently than anyone had thought.

The hit squad advanced on Qassim's car while it was stalled in a traffic jam. Then everything went wrong. The first assassin's pistol jammed and would not fire; the second assassin found that he had forgotten to load his gun; and the third assassin got his hand stuck in his pocket while trying to pull his hand grenade out. Impetuously, Saddam charged forward and opened fire on the president's car. He killed the driver and wounded the bodyguard, but Qassim had had enough warning to crouch on the floor, out of range. By this time the other members of the assassination squad had begun spraying bullets around, and the squad's leader was accidentally killed by one of his own men. Saddam and another man were wounded, also by their own side. Realizing that the assassination had become a bloody farce, the would-be killers fled, leaving Qassim to drive safely away.

The most significant thing about this bungled assassination attempt is the use that Saddam made of it in later years. He turned a disaster into a public-relations victory. According to his version of the assassination attempt, he was gravely wounded in a machine-gun battle with Qassim's men, gritted his teeth in stoic silence while a friend dug the bullet out of his leg with a razor blade, disguised himself as a desert tribesman, swam across the Tigris River, and then fled across the desert on a stolen horse to Syria to escape pursuit from Qassim's military patrols.

These remarkable feats were later immortalized in a propaganda movie about Saddam's life called *Aliyam Altawilah* ("The Long Days"). The film was designed by Saddam himself to glorify his deeds and enshrine him as a superhero. At a private screening of the film, an Egyptian journalist noticed that the actor who played Saddam only grimaced when the bullet was dug out. The journalist timidly suggested to Saddam that a scream or two might seem more realistic. Saddam proudly replied, "I did not think it was realistic either. I wanted the director to reshoot the scene because I remember the day when it happened. I did not grimace or move an inch until the bullet was out."[5]

All of this makes a good story, but it is not true. Not only was Saddam wounded by one of his own comrades instead of by Qassim's men, but Iraqi sources who were on the scene claim that the wound was not serious. Saddam and the other wounded Baathist were taken to an apartment, and a doctor was called to tend them; years later, the same doctor said that he found no bullet lodged in Saddam's leg. The midnight swim and the desperate gallop across the desert are also fictions, although warrants were issued for Saddam's arrest, and he did have to leave the country. He went to Tikrit and from there crossed the border into Syria—riding a donkey, according to some sources.

The attempt to kill Qassim had failed. But although the failure was a setback for the Baath party, Saddam managed to turn it into a personal triumph. By twisting the truth and rewriting history, he made himself look like a hero rather than a bungler. He continued to rewrite history in this self-serving way throughout his career. To Saddam Hussein, "truth" was whatever story served his purpose at the moment.

4

THE MASTER OF TERROR

AFTER LEAVING Iraq to escape arrest for his part in the attempt to kill President Qassim, Saddam Hussein spent three months in Damascus, the capital of Syria. There he was well received by high-ranking Baathists. Michel Aflaq, one of the Syrian founders of the Baath party, met and liked the young would-be assassin; afterward Aflaq helped Saddam to rise in the party's power structure.

In early 1960, Saddam moved on to Cairo, Egypt's capital and the center of pan-Arabist activity. He settled into a small apartment on the banks on the Nile River, in a district called Dukkie. The University of Cairo is located there, and the quarter had become the favored gathering place of student activists, political dissidents and exiles, and Arab nationalists. As a Baathist in exile for his pan-Arab activities, Saddam received an allowance from the Egyptian government; this enabled him to live in comfort, if not in style. He returned to school and, sometime in his early twenties, graduated from high school. Saddam's official biography says that in 1961 he enrolled in the Law Department of the University of Cairo, but his name does not appear in the university's records. Journalists Adel Darwish and Gregory Alexander, authors of *Unholy Babylon: The Secret History of Saddam's War*, claim that Saddam entered a small private college in Cairo at the age of twenty-three but failed to pass any of his exams.

During his stay in Cairo, Saddam ran into trouble with the law. On several occasions he was threatened with expulsion from the country for starting street fights. He was put in jail at least once, possibly twice; some sources say that he was suspected of murdering another Iraqi exile in a political argument. He was well known to the police in Dukkie as a troublemaker.

While living in Cairo, Saddam decided to marry. Marriages between cousins are common in Iraqi culture, and Saddam chose as a wife his cousin Sajidah, the daughter of his uncle Khayrallah, who agreed to the match. Some biographers say that Sajidah came to Cairo to marry Saddam; others say that the two became engaged, with the understanding that they would marry if and when Saddam was able to return to Iraq.

The chance to return came in February 1963, when a group of Baathist conspirators in Baghdad, with the support of some army officers, finally succeeded in overthrowing Qassim and taking control of Iraq's government. Saddam Hussein, still in Cairo, played no part in the coup. Qassim and his close associates were caught by surprise and executed while the army and the Baath militia battled Qassim's supporters in the streets. The Iraqi Communists put up a particularly determined fight against the Baathists, but in the end the Baath party carried the day.

Qassim had been popular with many Iraqis, and at first they refused to believe that he was dead. To convince the masses that Qassim had been executed, the Baathists turned to television. Samir al-Khalil, an Iraqi who fled the country to live abroad under an assumed name, gives a chilling account of the Baathist broadcast in his book *Republic of Fear: The Politics of Modern Iraq*:

> Night after night, they made their gruesome point. The body was propped up on a chair in the studio. A soldier sauntered around, handling its parts. The camera would cut to scenes of devastation at the Ministry of Defence where Qassim had made his last stand. There, on location, it lingered on the mutilated corpses of Qassim's entourage. . . . Back to the studio, and close-ups now of the entry and exit points of each bullet hole. The whole macabre sequence closes with a scene that must remain etched on the memory of all those who saw it: the soldier grabbed the lolling head by the hair, came right up close, and spat full face into it.[1]

As soon as he received word of the Baath triumph, Saddam Hussein hurried home from Egypt. If Saddam and Sajidah had not already gotten married, the ceremony took place upon Saddam's return, for they are known to have been married by mid-1963.

Saddam was happy to be back in Iraq. He looked forward to playing an important role in the new Baathist government. To his dismay, however, he found that the party leaders did not consider him a particularly important or impressive figure. He had been out of touch with the tangled internal politics of the Iraqi Baath party for more than three years; now he had to prove his worth to the new masters of Iraq. Fortunately, the man who had taken the post of prime minister after the coup, General Ahmad Hassan al-Bakr, was a fellow Tikriti. In fact, he was an older cousin of Saddam. By aligning himself with Bakr and a handful of other powerful Tikriti Baathists, Saddam strengthened his own position in the party. He also found a job: He was put in charge of interrogation and torture.

The February coup had killed between 1,500 and 5,000 people in a few days of open fighting, but the killing did not end there. Hundreds, perhaps thousands, more died in the weeks and months that followed. Baathist interrogation squads scoured the streets, armed with lists of "enemies" that they had carefully compiled before the coup. Anyone who crossed them was marked for arrest. The Iraqi Communists, in particular, suffered the Baathists' revenge for years of hostility between the two groups. Thousands of people associated in some way with the Iraq Communist party were arrested; hundreds were tortured and killed.

Saddam Hussein's terror squad set up its headquarters in a building called the Qasr-al-Nihayyat, which means the "Palace of the End." The palace got its name because it is where King Faisal II and his family were gunned down in Qassim's 1958 coup. To many trembling prisoners who entered the building in 1963, however, the name referred to the end of freedom, the end of hope, and often the end of life.

Saddam Hussein in an undated photo with his predecessor, General Ahmad Hassan al-Bakr. Hussein used his connection to Bakr, who was a cousin from Tikrit, to rise within the Baathist party.

Survivors of interrogation at Saddam's hands say that he enjoyed devising new torture methods and experimenting with them on prisoners. One of his favorite practices was to offer a victim a "menu," or list of possible tortures, from which the prisoner was forced to choose. One Iraqi who was imprisoned in the Qasr-al-Nihayyat in 1963 lived to tell how Saddam had treated him: "My hands and feet were tied together and I was hung by my feet from the ceiling. Saddam had converted a fan to take the weight of a man's body. As I was spun round, he beat me with a length of rubber hose filled with rubble."[2]

All the while, tension was growing within the Baath party. Baathist leaders, vying with one another for supremacy, could not agree on anything. One particularly bitter conflict involved competition between Syrian and Iraqi Baathists. Some Baathists felt that Syria, where the party had been born, should take the lead in all Baathist activities. According to this view, Baathist parties in other countries such as Iraq were merely "regional commands" of the Syrian-led central party. Many Baathists in Iraq, however, held a more nationalist view, declaring that Iraqi Baathism was an independent entity and that they would not take their orders from Syria. There were also disagreements between military and non-military Baathists. Dissension and factionalism widened into a split within the party, and at this moment of weakness the army stepped in and seized control. In November 1963, after only nine months in power, the Baath regime was overthrown. Saddam Hussein left the Qasr-al-Nihayyat in a hurry. Army officers who came to take control of the palace discovered the gruesome remains of his handiwork:

[When army officers reached the cellars of the Qasr-al-Nihayyat in 1963, they] found all sorts of loathsome instruments of torture, including electric wires with pincers, pointed iron stakes on which prisoners were made to sit, and a machine which still bore traces of chopped-off fingers. Small heaps of bloody clothing were scattered about and there were pools [of congealed blood] on the floor and [blood]stains all over the walls.[3]

The Baathists had lost control of Iraq, but they were by no means eliminated as a force within the country. Although party membership remained small—less than 1,000 members in the mid-1960s—the Baathists were determined to regain power. In early 1964, Saddam's cousin Bakr gained the secretary-generalship of the Iraqi Baath, the party's top position. Bakr made Saddam Hussein his deputy and put him in charge of security. Saddam was now able to carry out a plan he had cherished for months: the creation of a new secret police force for the party. He named it the Jihaz Haneen ("Instrument of Yearning"). All members of the Jihaz Haneen were Tikritis; most of them were Saddam's relatives by blood or marriage. Operating in secrecy and outside the law, the Jihaz Haneen soon became the most dreaded body of men in Iraq.

Saddam and his thugs systematically terrorized everyone who was thought to be a danger to Bakr's wing of the Baath. Even other Baathists were not safe; former colleagues who had split from Bakr were kidnapped, tortured, driven from the country, and in some cases killed. The Jihaz Haneen was especially severe on university students who were suspected of having Communist leanings. An Iraqi who was a first-year college student in 1966 later described the terror that Saddam inspired in a group of students who were holding a poetry reading. The reading was interrupted by screams, shots, and the sound of breaking glass, and then: "Someone put their head round the door and said one word, 'Saddam!' They all ran like hell for it."4

Saddam Hussein's reign of terror ended in October 1964, when he was picked up by the military government's security forces and sent to jail. Little is known for certain about the two years Saddam spent in prison. Saddam has given his own account, although it cannot be trusted. He claims that during his imprisonment he followed a strict routine of hard work, much reading, and frequent debate and discussion with his fellow inmates. Prison, in other words, only served to strengthen his leadership skills. Sajidah visited him every week, bringing Uday, their infant son. Saddam says that he kept in touch with Bakr by smuggling notes in and out of prison in Uday's clothing. In 1966, Saddam and another prisoner escaped from two guards who were taking them to court. Saddam went underground and resumed his terrorist activities. He also moved closer to the center of power in Baathist circles. Together with Bakr and a few other fellow Tikritis, he began plotting yet another coup.

They had a chance to begin their attack in late 1967, when crowds of Arab nationalists surged into the streets of Baghdad and other Iraqi cities. Egypt, Syria, and Jordan had just suffered a humiliating defeat in the Six Day War with Israel, and the crowds were angry that Iraq had not done more to help its Arab neighbors. The Baathists took advantage of this unrest to organize a series of anti-government strikes and protests.

The Baathists prepared for another coup, moving carefully to build up their power so that, after the coup, they would be able to control the army and other factions within the country. By July of 1968, the plotters were ready. With the aid of several high-ranking but rebellious army officers, they surrounded the palace, forced the frightened and ineffective president to sign a "resignation," and bundled him onto a plane bound for exile in London. The Baathists then went on radio and television to announce that they "had taken over power and ended the corrupt and weak regime."[5]

Baathist party propaganda calls this coup the "July revolution," but it was not a true revolution. The Baathist takeover was not a popular uprising with widespread support among the masses; rather, it was a carefully planned operation based on betrayal and furtively carried out. It did, however, make Saddam's cousin Bakr the new president of Iraq.

Saddam Hussein's role in the coup is not clear. He claims to have been in a tank that stormed the presidential palace, but some witnesses say that by the time Saddam and a gang of his half-brothers from the Jihaz Haneen arrived on the scene, the former president had already surrendered. As the Baath security chief, Saddam was in charge of mopping up any resistance to the new regime. He performed this task with ruthless efficiency. Soon Bakr's enemies had disappeared—they were jailed, killed, exiled, or driven underground.

As Bakr settled into the presidency, Saddam Hussein assumed the role of his cousin's second-in-command. As the second most powerful man in the country and in the Baath party, he coined the title Deputy Secretary-General and insisted upon being addressed as "Mr. Deputy." He expanded his secret police into a national internal-security force with himself as its head, and he continued to cultivate the reputation for terror and cruelty that had made him universally feared. Over time, he came to dominate Bakr, gradually cutting the president off from other supporters and isolating him inside a circle of security guards who were loyal only to Saddam. Within a few years, President Bakr had become a powerless figurehead. Saddam Hussein was the real strongman of Iraq.

5

"LONG LIVE SADDAM!"

DURING THE 1970s, Saddam Hussein hid himself in the role of "Mr. Deputy." Although it is likely that Saddam wanted to shove Bakr aside and become president himself, Bakr was popular with most of the senior Baathists. He was also well liked by the army officers, who respected him because he had had a military career. In the first years of Baathist rule, Saddam was not ready to challenge Bakr openly. He kept out of the public eye and concentrated on building his strength behind the scenes.

Saddam also acquired a set of false credentials. In 1972 he enrolled in law school at the University of Baghdad, saying that as he had attended law classes in Cairo, he did not need to attend them in Baghdad. All he wanted to do was take the test to receive his law degree. University officials agreed to let him take the test. On the appointed day, as the story goes, he showed up in a military-style uniform, accompanied by armed bodyguards, and slapped a pistol down onto his desk—

"to make me feel more comfortable," he explained. He passed the test. Four years later he arranged for the university to grant him a master's degree in law.

Similarly, Saddam had always resented the fact that he had not been able to attend the military academy. He also feared that his lack of military experience put him at a disadvantage against other top party officials and Arab nationalist leaders, most of whom were army officers. By 1976, however, he had become so powerful that he could simply declare himself an officer. He gave himself the rank of lieutenant general and on many occasions wore snappy military uniforms, festooned with braid and glittering with badges. Later, after he became president, he promoted himself to the rank of field marshal.

Rumors said that Saddam Hussein's favorite film was *The Godfather*, a classic story of life in an American organized crime family. Certainly Saddam behaved like the "Godfather." His values and attitudes, as well as those of the people closest to him, mirrored those of the movie's gangsters: brutality, constant suspicion and fear of betrayal, greed, and flamboyant corruption. The greed and corruption emerged early in the Baathist regime.

Once he felt secure in his power, Saddam began raising money in a variety of ways. One of his most successful ventures was the reintroduction of horse racing into Iraq. Racing had been banned under Qassim because it was associated with gambling, which was forbidden by Islam. Saddam, however, allowed the race tracks to reopen—for a fee. Some of the money that Saddam raised was used to fund his security operations, but some was hidden away in overseas bank accounts earmarked for Saddam and his family.

Saddam's relatives and fellow Tikritis took advantage of his prominence to advance themselves. In addition to holding public offices, where they had the chance to enrich themselves by taking bribes and embezzling public funds, many family members branched out into business. A cousin named Hussein Kamel al-Majid received a "personal commission" of $60 million for helping to arrange the purchase of 120 missiles from China. Hussein's son Uday made millions by illegally selling foreign money, such as U.S. dollars, on the black market—transactions that were approved by his father. Perhaps the most notorious of the Tikritis, though, was Khayrallah Tulfah, Saddam's uncle, who was appointed mayor of Baghdad when the Baathists came to power. Through a combination of threats, illegal seizures, and political favor-trading, he acquired most of the citrus-growing land in Iraq, giving him control of the country's citrus industry. No one dared to stand up to him, for behind him loomed the terrible shadow of Saddam Hussein and the Jihaz Haneen. Eventually, however, Khayrallah's rampant corruption became too embarrassing even for Saddam, who removed him from his post as mayor.

Few details are known of Saddam Hussein's family life. He remained married to Sajidah, and they had five children: two sons, Uday and Qusai, and three daughters, Raghad, Rana, and Hala. There were, however, other women in Saddam's life. The best known of these relationships occurred after Saddam became president and involved a prominent woman in Baghdad society, Samira Shahbandar, who is said by some sources to have become his second wife (Islam permits a man to have as many as four wives). This relationship brought much strife to Saddam's household. His son Uday, feeling

In a photo (from the Matar biography) taken sometime after he took over as president, Saddam poses with his eldest son Uday. He wears the uniform of a field marshal, a self-appointed ranking.

The Hussein family, in 1990. Seated
on the couch are Saddam's wife,
Sajida, and his third daughter, Hala.
Uday stands in the middle with Rana
to the left of him and Raghad,
carrying her baby, to the right.
Qusai stands at the far right.

that his father's affair with Samira Shahbandar was an insult to his mother, killed the servant of Saddam's who had brought Saddam and the woman together. The murder, which was not Uday's first, was brutal and highly public.[1] Furious, Saddam had Uday jailed and threatened to kill him. Uday was later exiled to Switzerland for a few years, although his father eventually allowed him to return to Iraq and restored him to favor.

Saddam not only punished anyone who criticized him, but he also took swift and ruthless revenge on those who gossiped about his family. Omar al-Hazzah, a general from Tikrit, happened to remark while visiting the home of a woman friend that he had once had a sexual relationship with Saddam's mother. Unknown to either the general or his friend, the woman's home had been bugged by Saddam's secret police, and Saddam heard a tape of the conversation. The woman, the general, and the general's son were executed; their homes were bulldozed to the ground. Harsh incidents like this one created an aura of fear and awe around Saddam. His eyes and ears were everywhere; no one could be sure of escaping his wrath.

★ ★ ★

SADDAM HUSSEIN served as the deputy secretary-general of Iraq at an eventful and important time in the Arab world. The concerns of the 1970s would affect Saddam Hussein's actions later, when he became the president of Iraq. One of these concerns was Israel: During the 1970s, the Middle East was wracked with conflict over the question of Israel's right to exist and the fate of the Palestinian Arabs. Another concern was oil, which played a key part in the region's political life at that time. Middle Eastern petroleum was a subject of great concern to many people around the world, from Arab sheikhs and oil ministers to Americans waiting in long lines at gas stations.

Petroleum, or oil, had been known since ancient times to exist in many parts of the Middle East. In places it welled up from underground to form sticky asphalt pools. In the twentieth century, oil came into demand as fuel and as raw material for the plastics and petrochemical industries. Companies were hastily formed in Britain, the United States, and other industrialized nations to search for oil around the world. Suddenly the barren deserts of the Middle East were valuable. On either side of the Persian Gulf—especially in Iran, Iraq, Kuwait, and Saudi Arabia—the sands were found to conceal some of the world's largest reserves of oil.

Western companies began drilling wells and pumping oil in the Persian Gulf region, and by the 1950s the region had become one of the world's leading producers and exporters of oil. The companies leased the right to pump and export the oil in exchange for paying a fee, or for giving a share of the profits over to the host country. Enormous amounts of cash flowed into the Gulf states. In the space of just a few years, places such as Saudi Arabia were transformed from poor, almost medieval sheikhdoms into rich nations. The rapid pace of change and westernization created social and cultural stresses as a single generation leaped from the camel to the Lear jet. And although the Gulf states used their oil revenues to build airports, schools, hospitals, and other facilities to improve people's lives, a substantial share of the oil money made its way into the personal fortunes of ruling families and government leaders, causing discontent among the poorer folk. Furthermore, although the Gulf states earned millions of dollars for their oil, the foreign companies that exported it were making billions. Many people in Iran, Iraq, and the other oil-producing countries felt that they, and not the foreign oil companies, should get the larger share of the profits.

After World War II, nationalism replaced colonialism as the driving force in the Middle East. The domination of the Western powers waned. With independence came the desire for full ownership and control of natural resources, especially oil. Iran took action in 1951 and nationalized its oil industry. Iran's government announced that the foreign oil leases were ended and bought the drilling equipment and installations from the furious oil companies. Iraq followed, nationalizing its oil industry in 1972. Kuwait, which had gained independence from Britain in 1961, did the same in 1975.

In 1960, thirteen of the world's oil-producing nations had formed the Organization of Petroleum Exporting Countries, usually called OPEC. Iran, Iraq, Saudi Arabia, and Kuwait were members. Some nations outside the Arab world, such as Venezuela, belonged to OPEC, but neither the United States nor any other major industrial power was included. OPEC exercised considerable power over the world supply of oil. At OPEC meetings, oil ministers from the member nations tried to reach the right balance between production and prices. If too much oil was pumped, the supply of oil went up, and the price per barrel went down. On the other hand, if production was cut back, the supply was reduced, and prices went up, meaning higher profits for the OPEC countries. High prices could backfire, though. If they became *too* high, big energy consumers such as the United States and Japan might start conserving energy or developing solar, wind, or nuclear power. OPEC tried to keep people buying oil at the best possible prices by setting production quotas for each member country; OPEC also set the price at which a barrel of crude oil could be sold.

Dissension frequently occurred within OPEC. Member nations argued often about production levels, and some were known to cheat by producing more oil than their quotas allowed. Oil was at the bottom of some border disputes in the Middle East, as well. Iraq became embroiled in several conflicts of this type. One concerned the Rumaila oilfield, which lies beneath the Iraq-Kuwait border and is divided between the two countries. Iraq repeatedly accused Kuwait of taking more than its share of oil from this field by drilling slanted wells along the border to tap into Iraq's underground oil reserves.

Iraq was also at a disadvantage in regard to the ports and shipping lanes needed to transport oil out of the country. The borders drawn by the British gave the good harbors to Kuwait. Iraq's coastline on the Persian Gulf is very short and is blocked from easy access to the Gulf by two islands, Warba and Bubaiyan, that belong to Kuwait. Iraq demanded that Kuwait hand over the islands so an Iraqi oil terminal could be built there, but Kuwait indignantly refused. This left Iraq with only one useful outlet to the shipping lanes of the Gulf: the Shatt-al-Arab waterway, which is formed by the meeting of the Tigris and Euphrates rivers near Basra and flows into the Persian Gulf. The Shatt-al-Arab, however, lies along the Iran-Iraq border. The waterway was divided between the two countries, but they quarreled repeatedly over where the border should be drawn in

the channel. Iran's dominance in the Shatt-al-Arab became a deep grievance to Iraq, for while Iran has other
ports on its long coastline, Iraq is dependent upon the
Shatt-al-Arab. With so little access to the sea, Iraq was
forced to invest in costly, vulnerable pipelines to carry
its oil to ports in Syria, Turkey, and Saudi Arabia.

Saddam Hussein learned a valuable lesson about
the power of oil in October 1973. When war broke out
between Israel and the Arab nations of Egypt and Syria,
the Islamic oil-producing countries banned the sale of
petroleum to Israel and its supporters, including the
United States. This ban touched off the most severe
energy crisis in history. The United States, where energy use per person is the highest in the world, was
especially hard hit. As winter approached, people piled
on sweaters and turned their thermostats down, mind-
ful of shortages of heating oil. Gasoline was rationed,
and drivers had to wait for hours in lines at filling
stations. There was talk of developing solar and wind
power to reduce America's dependence on foreign oil.
Like other leaders of the Arab states, Saddam saw that
oil could be used as a weapon against the energy-
hungry nations of the West.

Another development in the Persian Gulf region
during the 1970s became a source of trouble for Saddam. This development was the rise of Islamic fundamentalism in Iran. The shah, or king, of Iran was an ally
of the United States. He had brought a high degree of
modernization and westernization to his country, although his regime was corrupt and repressive. During
the 1970s he came under increasing criticism from a
group of Muslim clerics who wanted the country to be
governed in strict accordance with traditional Islamic
law. The leader of this Islamic fundamentalist move-

ment was the Ayatollah Ruhollah Khomeini, who was exiled from Iran for agitating the people against the shah. Khomeini took refuge in Iraq for a time. He became so popular with the Shiites of Iraq that Saddam expelled him, fearing that Khomeini would incite the Iraqi Shiites—who were already at odds with the mostly Sunni Baath party—to rise up against the Baathist regime.

★　★　★

ALL THIS TIME, events inside Iraq were careening along on a course of repression and bloodshed. When the Baathists came to power in 1968, they introduced some reforms that benefited the Iraqi people. They made education and health care available to more people than ever before, and they continued the policy of land reform that Qassim had begun. These reforms won a wide measure of support for the Baath, especially among the poorer people of the cities and the countryside, who were grateful for the improvements in their standard of living. Many educated Iraqis, too, at first hailed the Baath for bringing pan-Arabism to Iraq. But the party also brought a reign of terror and persecution. From the start, Saddam Hussein was associated with this darker side of Baathism.

As soon as the Baathists came to power, they cracked down on every group within the country that could possibly pose a threat to their rule. With President Bakr's support, Saddam Hussein masterminded a series of purges—waves of arrest and punishment designed to get rid of "enemies." Some victims of the purges undoubtedly *were* enemies of the Baath regime. They were spies, conspirators, or simply outspoken critics of Baathism. Most victims of the purges, how-

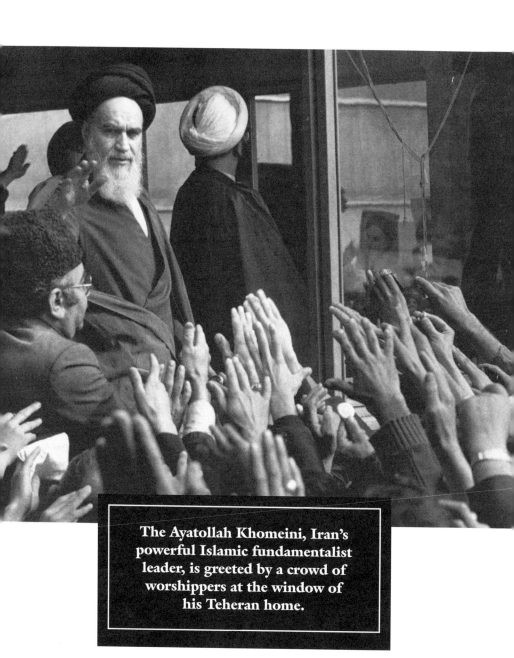

The Ayatollah Khomeini, Iran's
powerful Islamic fundamentalist
leader, is greeted by a crowd of
worshippers at the window of
his Teheran home.

ever, were guilty only of belonging to a group that Saddam had targeted. He used the purges to give the Baath party a stranglehold on Iraq by removing all non-Baathists from important positions, by crushing all dissent or opposition, and by creating an atmosphere of suspicion and terror that would make people afraid to plot against him or even to criticize him.

The first purge was aimed at the country's remaining Jews. In January 1969, fourteen people, including the head of Iraq's Jewish community, were arrested as spies for Israel. After farcical trials, they were publicly hanged in "Liberation Square," as the Baathists renamed one of Baghdad's large plazas. The hangings were broadcast live on television, and people were urged to come to Baghdad to witness the deaths of these "enemies" of the Arab cause. Some families picnicked in a park while they watched the executions, but most of the several hundred thousand Iraqis who attended the hangings formed a dancing, stone-throwing mob that cried "Death to the spies!" and "Death to the traitors!" at every fresh victim. To the cheering crowd, a Baathist government minister promised, "This is only the beginning! The great and immortal squares of Iraq shall be filled up with the corpses of traitors and spies! Just wait!"[2]

They did not have to wait long. Twenty more Jews were hanged later that year, accused of being Israeli spies. The new rulers of Iraq discovered that by claiming to have exposed "spy networks" they could kill two birds with one stone: They could eliminate their opponents and at the same time win the applause of the masses. Purges against Jews were especially popular with the crowds because of the strong anti-Israel feeling among the Arab peoples. Once the purges began, however, a number of Jews fled the country, leaving only a tiny remnant of the ancient Jewish community.

Throughout Bakr's presidency, Saddam and the other Baathists relentlessly purged politicians, student activists, and army officers. Anyone who criticized the Baath party or who might develop a popular following was targeted for elimination; Baathism would tolerate no rivals. Sometimes the victims were arrested on trumped-up criminal or espionage charges and given mock trials. Cruelly, their families were required to pay for the bullets with which they were executed. Often, however, victims were simply picked up at home or on the street by the security police and never seen again. Later, their relatives might be shown a sealed coffin and told that the victim died of an illness or accident. Bodies were never available for examination, which suggests that the victims were tortured and brutalized.

Purges were carried out vigorously against the groups that traditionally had battled the Baathists. Saddam Hussein persuaded Bakr to adopt a treacherous stance toward the Communists. Bakr offered the Iraqi Communist party a truce and a share in government power; this gesture enabled Iraq to buy arms from the Soviet Union, the patron of the Communists. But on the very day that Bakr signed the peace treaty with Iraq's Communist leaders, Saddam distributed to the Jihaz Haneen a pamphlet titled "How to Destroy the Iraqi Communist Party." He went on to oversee the killing of hundreds of Communist supporters.

The Shiites, too, were purged. Saddam was afraid that Iraq's Shiites, who made up the majority of the population, would unite under a strong leader as the Iranians were uniting under Khomeini. He was also jealous of the adoration shown by the masses toward

Shiite religious leaders. He therefore produced "evidence" that the son of Iraq's most respected Shiite cleric was a spy for Iran; the son was eventually assassinated by the Jihaz Haneen. From then on, Shiite leaders refrained from public appearances and stayed out of Saddam's way.

Saddam and other Arab nationalists felt a special loathing for the Kurds. In 1969, when Kurdish guerrillas attacked the oil wells near Kirkuk, which is in Kurdish territory, the army's response was swift and savage. Two-thirds of the nation's fighting force were sent into the mountainous north to pound Kurdish settlements into rubble. The Kurds describe an atrocity committed near the village of Dakan as typical of the horrors of this ethnic war:

> The children and the women of the village escaped to one of the caves in the vicinity, for fear of artillery shelling and bombing by aircraft.
> After burning the village, the officers and mercenaries assembled near the entry of the cave. They collected wood, and after sprinkling the wood with petrol [gasoline], they set fire to it. The cries of the children and the women began rising to God. They were shooting at the entry of the cave so that no one could escape, and so were burnt 67 children and women in the cave.[3]

Despite the violence of the fighting in 1969, Bakr and Saddam did not want to wage all-out war on the Kurds. They knew that such a war would be prolonged and costly, and they feared that it might weaken Iraq and make it vulnerable to attack from outside. Over the next few years, the Baathists tried several times to arrange peace terms with the Kurds. Each time, however, the Kurds insisted on self-rule and the control of the Kirkuk oilfields. The government was unwilling to meet these terms, so negotiations always broke down and the fighting started anew. Entire Kurdish towns were wiped out. The Baathists also drove many Kurds out of the country. Between 1972 and 1975, several hundred thousand Kurds were stripped of their property and deported to Turkey and Iran. Others were forcibly relocated to the deserts of southern Iraq, where they were dispersed among Arab villages and forbidden to form their own communities.

Even the Baathists were not immune from the purges. Saddam did not hesitate to destroy colleagues who set themselves up as rivals or blocked his path to supreme power. On at least one occasion, Saddam himself was almost eliminated. Nadhim Kazzar was Saddam's right-hand man and the head of his internal-security police. Noted for his brutality—he was said to enjoy putting out cigarettes in prisoners' eyes—he was one of Saddam's closest associates outside his own family. Kazzar was hungry for more power, however, and in 1973 he plotted to assassinate both Bakr and Saddam. The plot failed, and Kazzar and his fellow conspirators were executed, making Saddam more secure than ever in his position as the behind-the-scenes ruler of Iraq.

By 1979, Saddam Hussein was ready to step into the spotlight. Tired of playing second-in-command to his cousin Bakr, he adopted the title "the Leader," began making public appearances, and had huge posters of himself plastered on walls all over Iraq. Other members of the government warned Bakr that Saddam was preparing to move against him. But Saddam, who had had his security police secretly install listening devices in his colleagues' offices and homes, forestalled their attempts to unite against him. In July 1979, on the anniversary of the coup that had brought the Baathists to power, Saddam announced that President Bakr had resigned the day before because of poor health. (In reality, Bakr was under house arrest. He quietly retired to private life and died a few years later.) Saddam also declared that he had been chosen by the Baath party as Iraq's new president, commander in chief, and head of government, as well as leader of the party.

The new president inaugurated his administration with the most spectacular purge yet. He gathered nearly a thousand high-ranking Baathists and government officials in a large meeting hall, ordered guards to seal the doors, and then revealed that he had learned of a plot against him and against the party. He produced several of the alleged conspirators. In dazed, monotone voices these "witnesses" read "confessions" that told how they had conspired to overthrow Saddam and the Baath party. (Saddam's security police were holding the families of the "confessors" hostage.) With tears streaming down his face, Saddam asked the audience, "What am I to do with traitors such as these?" The audience gave the expected reply: "Death to traitors!"

Saddam then told his listeners that the conspiracy was widespread, and that he had a complete list of the plotters. He proceeded to scan a list of party members; anyone whose name he called was removed by the guards. Tension became almost unbearable as Saddam moved slowly down the list. Eyewitnesses say that some men fainted with relief when he passed over their names. All the while, a guard filmed the scene with a video camera. The tape was later circulated as a warning to anyone who might think about double-crossing Saddam.

By the time the meeting ended, more than fifty men had been led from the room. The survivors broke into frenzied shouts of "Long live Saddam! Long live Saddam!" The execution of the "traitors" a few days later had a uniquely personal touch. Saddam forced senior party members to join him in the firing squad that killed the prisoners. Even those who had unquestioningly accepted the earlier purges sensed that Iraq had now descended to a new level of terror and violence. The era of Saddam Hussein had officially begun.

THE NEW NEBUCHADNEZZAR

ONE OF Saddam Hussein's first acts as president of Iraq was to plunge the country into a long, costly war with its neighbor Iran—the latest chapter in the age-old history of bitter conflict between the two lands.

Trouble began brewing with the rise of the Shiite fundamentalist movement in Iran. Some Iraqi Shiite leaders called for a similar movement in Iraq, while across the border the Iranians urged their fellow Shiites in Iraq to rise up against the Baathist government. In 1979, Iran's fundamentalists overthrew the shah of Iran and installed a new government headed by the Ayatollah Khomeini, who announced that Iran would spread the fundamentalist revolution throughout the Islamic world. Khomeini also wanted to end secular Baathist rule in Iraq and to drive the "infidel" Saddam Hussein out of office. Iran began trying to topple Saddam's government indirectly, by providing aid to Iraqi Shiite and Kurdish insurrectionists and also by making terrorist attacks. In early 1980 at least twenty Iraqi officials were assassinated by the Shiite underground. A Shiite bomb nearly killed Tariq Aziz, Saddam's foreign minister.

Saddam tried to quell the wave of Shiite unrest with threats and purges. When that failed, he tried to win over the Shiites by proclaiming his own spiritual piety. He even produced an elaborate family tree that "proved" that he was descended from the prophet Muhammad as well as the caliph Ali, revered by the Shiites. Both the Iranians and the underground Iraqi Shiite movement, however, remained firmly opposed to Saddam and to Baathism. Saddam responded by executing hundreds of Shiite leaders and expelling some 80,000 Shiites from the country.

In the summer of 1980, tensions mounted along the Iran-Iraq border. Raids and artillery attacks broke out. Saddam decided that the best way to deal with this persistent threat was with a direct assault. He declared war on Iran and, with half of the Iraqi armed forces, launched an attack on southwestern Iran. His goal, he announced, was not to overthrow Khomeini's government but merely to take control of the Shatt-al-Arab waterway and of Khuzistan, an Iranian region with a mostly Arab population.

Saddam made two grave miscalculations. First, he assumed that the war would be over in two or three weeks—that Iran, weakened by revolution, would crumble before his assault. He could not have been more wrong. Second, he insisted on directing Iraq's military strategy and battle plans himself, despite his complete lack of military experience. Generals at the front were forced to wait for orders from Saddam before they could take any action; Saddam wanted everyone to know that he was in charge. He also transferred high-ranking officers frequently to prevent a popular general from building a following that might threaten Saddam's rule. As a result, Iraq's armed forces were less effective than they might have been.

In the first weeks of the war, Iraq gained the upper hand, capturing some territory inside the Iranian border. But when the Iraqi army tried to push on toward Abadan, a strategic Iranian city on the Shatt-al-Arab, they were halted by a vigorous Iranian defense. Soon both sides had settled into trenches. The campaign that Saddam had hoped to conclude in a few weeks turned into an agonizing, long-drawn-out war of attrition. Iran had several advantages. For one thing, it was three times the size of Iraq, with a larger population. Furthermore, Iran viewed the conflict as a religious war, a holy crusade. Iranian clerics convinced the masses that anyone who died fighting Iraq would go straight to heaven as a martyr for the glorious Islamic cause. Soldiers, hearing this, became filled with religious exaltation. Thus arose the phenomenon of Iran's "human wave" assaults, in which thousands of poorly armed soldiers, some of them as young as twelve years of age, charged Iraqi tanks and trenches, heedless of the fact that they were running toward almost certain death. In some cases the Iranian troops ran across the bodies of their fallen comrades, right up to the muzzles of Iraqi guns.

Although Iraq scored an initial success, Saddam Hussein failed to order the military to follow up with an all-out assault on Teheran, the capital of Iran. Had he done so, the war might indeed have ended quickly. But the Iraqi troops halted in Khuzistan, giving the Iranians time to muster their strength. Soon a series of Iranian counterattacks had turned the tide of battle against Iraq. By the end of 1981, part of the Iraqi occupying

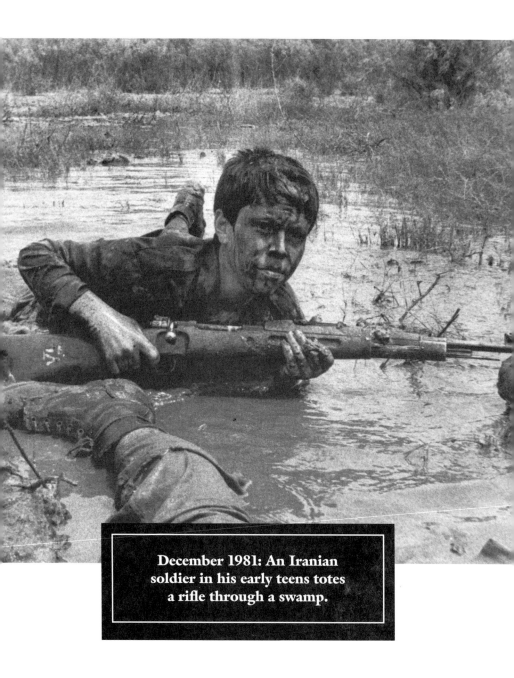

December 1981: An Iranian
soldier in his early teens totes
a rifle through a swamp.

force had been driven out of Khuzistan and back across the border.

Having failed to achieve his goals, Saddam Hussein offered to call off the war. But Iran was motivated by religious fanaticism, not by practical goals; Khomeini turned down Saddam's offer and stepped up the attack. In May 1982 the Iraqis were driven out of Khorramshahr, an Iranian city they had seized early in the war. Terrified by the Iranian onslaught, the Iraqis fled the battlefield, leaving behind most of their weapons and thousands of troops as prisoners of war.

The war was two years old. Approximately 100,000 Iraqis had died; Iranian casualties were at least as high, although published figures are unreliable. Again Saddam offered peace. Again Iran refused. The Iranians now carried the attack into Iraq, launching an assault on Basra, Iraq's second-largest city. The Iraqi armed forces put up a spirited defense and halted the Iranian advance near the border. There for a time matters remained stalemated. The war ground on unendingly, with neither side gaining much territory despite the steadily mounting death toll on both sides. The United Nations tried to arrange a cease-fire agreement. Iraq agreed to the UN proposal, but Iran rejected it.

★ ★ ★

IRAQ HAD entered the war with a powerful armory of weapons; for years, the country had been stockpiling military equipment bought from other nations. During the 1970s, the Soviet Union was Iraq's main supplier of weaponry. In the 1980s, Saddam Hussein began obtaining military supplies from Western nations. France was Iraq's chief Western supplier, but Iraq also bought munitions from Japan, West Germany, Portugal, Belgium, Spain, and Brazil. These purchases included not only conventional weapons but also the materials needed to make chemical and nuclear weapons. The United States did not sell weapons to Iraq; starting in 1984, however, the United States supplied Saddam with financial aid and military intelligence information. American policy-makers hoped that by aiding Saddam they would keep Khomeini's Iran from becoming the supreme power in the Persian Gulf.

Saddam had hoped to make Iraq militarily superior to the other Gulf nations by doing what no other Arab nation had done: acquiring nuclear weapons. In the late 1970s he had bought a nuclear reactor from France and began building the Osiraq power plant. Although Hussein claimed the reactor was for research, experts pointed out that the equipment was bigger than necessary for scientific purposes but could easily produce nuclear warheads. Iraq's neighbors dreaded this possibility. Soon after the Iran-Iraq war began, Iran tried to destroy Osiraq but failed. An Israeli air bombardment eliminated the plant in 1981.

Saddam was thwarted in his nuclear ambitions, but he had other weapons at his disposal. Several times during the 1980s he used chemical weapons, even though the Geneva Convention, a set of international agreements on the conduct of war, outlaws such weapons. The army used napalm, a chemical that burns and blinds, against Kurdish insurrectionists in the north. Saddam also employed mustard gas, cyanide, and nerve gas against Iranian troops as early as 1982. The most notorious cases of chemical warfare, though, occurred in the late 1980s, when the Iraqi army, under the command of one of Saddam's cousins, quelled a large Kurdish uprising in the northern mountains. In

Iraqi gunners fire at the Iranian
cities of Abadan and Khorramshahr.
Iraq bought arms from the Soviets in
the 1970s. As the war dragged on into
the 1980s, Hussein turned to Western
powers for financial aid and materials
to make nuclear and chemical weapons.

addition to executing Kurdish prisoners of war, bull-dozing whole towns and villages, and putting half a million Kurds in concentration camps, the army gassed several dozen Kurdish villages. The worst atrocity was in March 1988. Iraqi planes, perhaps by mistake, gassed the Kurdish town of Halabja, killing 5,000 people and injuring twice that number in a single day.

The Israeli bombing of Osiraq and the war against the Kurds took place against the backdrop of unrelenting conflict with Iran. For the people of Iraq, war seemed to have become a permanent way of life. During the first few years of the war, Saddam Hussein was able to keep the majority of Iraqis fairly contented. Casualties were high, but the government paid a large benefit—cash, a car, and land—to the families of soldiers killed in battle. Consumer goods remained plentiful; there were no food shortages. As time went on, however, the mood of the public darkened. By the mid-1980s it seemed that every family in Iraq had lost a brother, husband, or son. Food and other goods grew scarce and expensive, and most people had little money—almost no one had received a pay raise since before the start of the war.

Saddam was forced to seek outside aid for Iraq's economy and war effort. The Shatt-al-Arab had been closed to navigation since the war began. Syria, which allied with Iran against its rival for the leadership of Baathism, refused to let Iraq use its highways or oil pipelines. Saddam had to turn to Kuwait, Jordan, and Turkey for transport routes in and out of Iraq. The leaders of these nations were willing to help Iraq because they were terrified that Khomeini's revolution might spread to their countries and topple their regimes. Throughout the Iran-Iraq war, the Arab nations helped Saddam because he seemed to be a barrier protecting them from the fanatical excesses of Islamic fundamentalism.

Iraq also received support from the United States, even though the two countries had been on unfriendly terms before the war broke out. The United States had stopped giving foreign aid to Iraq because Iraq harbored terrorists who were responsible for attacks on American civilians. However, Saddam made the gesture of expelling one terrorist, the notorious Abu Nidal, opening the way for U.S. aid to Iraq in the form of cash, food supplies, and weapons. American officials still disliked and distrusted Saddam, but they feared Khomeini even more. They decided to back Saddam because he seemed the lesser of two evils. Geoffrey Kemp, a national-security official under President Ronald Reagan, explained: "It wasn't that we wanted Iraq to win the war—we did not want Iraq to lose."[1] A victory for Iran and Khomeini, who reviled the United States as the "Great Satan," was unthinkable to American foreign-policy strategists.

As the war dragged on year after year, Saddam had to use extreme measures to control the growing discontent of the Iraqi populace. One of his methods was to fill Iraq with his own image. Newspapers and magazines, which were censored by the party, were almost exclusively devoted to coverage of "the Leader's" every word and action. His portrait appeared in every schoolroom, every office, every public place, and many private homes. Visitors to the country joked that Iraq's population was 28 million: 14 million Iraqis and 14 million pictures of Saddam Hussein. Giant billboards and murals of Saddam sprouted in every city and town. Some showed him as a war hero, in military uniform; some

Hussein responded to Iraqi dismay at ever-mounting casualties on the Iranian front by having giant propaganda murals and billboards plastered on the sides of buildings, along highways, and in public places throughout the nation.

showed him praying, or with his family, or leading a rebuilt Iraq toward a golden future.

Many of these images portrayed Saddam Hussein against a background of ancient palaces and monuments, symbols of Iraq's glorious Babylonian past. Just as he had claimed to be a descendant of Muhammad, founder of Islam, Saddam also claimed to be the modern heir of Nebuchadnezzar and other Mesopotamian heroes. Each year on his birthday, which he had made a national holiday, he ordered elaborate spectacles, such as a laser light show that etched huge, glowing portraits of Saddam and Nebuchadnezzar side by side in the night sky. He started a reconstruction of the ancient city of Babylon with bricks marked, "The Babylon of Nebuchadnezzar was rebuilt in the era of Saddam Hussein," and he promised a prize of $1.5 million to any architect who could re-create the fabled "hanging gardens" of old Babylon. Saddam felt that Iraq's historical importance entitled it to be a leader among the nations of the Middle East. One reason for his attack on Iran had been to prove that Iraq, not Iran, was the supreme power in the Gulf region.

Saddam Hussein has often been compared with Adolf Hitler of Germany and Joseph Stalin of Russia. Both created totalitarian societies in which every aspect of life was dominated by the state, and the state was dominated by one man. Saddam forged a similar totalitarianism in Iraq. Like Hitler, he used a vast system of spies and informers. Criticizing the government, or even making jokes about "the Leader," became a crime that carried the death penalty. Careless words met with harsh reprisals. Once, while visiting a school, Saddam apparently asked a boy, "Do you know who I am?" The boy unwarily replied, "Yes, you are the man who makes my father curse whenever you come on television." The boy and his family disappeared; their house was bulldozed into nothingness. Anecdotes about such incidents created a mood of universal fear, mistrust, and suspicion. People were urged to turn in neighbors, co-workers, or family members who spoke against the state. One foreign journalist reported after visiting Iraq that the country consisted of three million people spying on the other eleven million.[2]

Saddam also resembled Hitler in his attack on the traditional family. According to the Baathist view that Saddam promoted, a child was the property of the state and should be brainwashed with the state's values from an early age. Children were funneled into youth organizations, clubs, camps, and rallies that turned them into ardent young Baathists. They were also trained to spy on their parents. Saddam said, "You must place in every corner a son of the revolution, with a trustworthy eye and a firm mind that receives its instructions from the responsible centre of the revolution."[3]

Civil rights had always been precarious in Iraq, but during the war they were almost completely eroded. Political parties could not be formed; meetings and assemblies were banned unless sponsored by the Baath party; freedom of the press was nonexistent. Contact with the outside world was cut off. Iraqis were forbidden to leave the country, to receive foreign newspapers, or to talk with foreigners. Amnesty International, an organization that collects information about human-rights abuses from around the world, reported that each year thousands of Iraqis were jailed without formal charges. People learned not to question the sudden, unexplained disappearance of a colleague or neighbor. Some of the victims returned, much shaken, to their families and jobs, but hundreds of others were tortured and executed.

Saddam's supporters liked to point out areas in which his rule was progressive. For example, he built many schools in rural, underdeveloped parts of Iraq. This progress was undercut, however, by the fact that all schools were tools of the party. Education was seen as an opportunity to indoctrinate young people, and critical thinking and the free expression of ideas were not permitted. Similarly, although women in traditional Islamic societies are subordinate to their male relatives, with few independent rights, the founders of the Baath party supported equal rights for women. Saddam passed laws allowing women to work, to divorce their husbands, and to own property. But later, when he needed the support of the more traditional element in the population, he reversed himself, passing a law that echoed medieval Islamic tradition: A man could kill any female relative—wife, mother, sister, aunt, cousin— who committed adultery, and the killing would not be considered a crime.

Several attempts were made on Saddam's life during the war. His narrow escapes from assassination deepened Saddam's belief that he was surrounded by conspirators and enemies. He moved quickly to crush anyone who appeared to be gaining power or popularity. Generals who won battles against Iran disappeared from public view; some of them are thought to have been executed. Even Saddam's cousin and oldest friend, Adnan Khayrallah, began to seem like a threat. Saddam had made him defense minister but was annoyed that Adnan was popular with the Iraqi public. In addition, the two men quarreled over Saddam's harsh treatment of his son Uday. In 1989, Adnan Khayrallah was killed when his helicopter crashed in the desert. His death appeared accidental, but observers note that a suspicious number of Saddam's opponents have met their deaths in helicopter crashes.

The war took a new turn in 1986 when Iran captured the Fao Peninsula on Iraq's coastline. This gave Iran almost total control over the shipping in the northern part of the Persian Gulf. Fearing attacks from Iran, Kuwait sought protection for its oil tankers, and both the United States and the Soviet Union allowed Kuwaiti ships to fly their flags. American, British, and French ships and troops were sent to police the Gulf. The Americans were drawn into the conflict in 1987, when an Iraqi plane fired a missile that struck the U.S.S. *Stark*, killing thirty-seven sailors. Iraq apologized, saying that its pilot had mistaken the *Stark* for an Iranian ship, and paid compensation to the dead men's families. From that time, however, the United States took a more direct role in the war. Although the United States did not declare war on Iran, American forces patrolling the Gulf sank or disabled a large part of Iran's fleet.

The tide of war now turned against Iran. The Iraqi army recaptured the Fao Peninsula, and demoralized Iranian soldiers fled the battlefields in disarray. Iran's will to fight had weakened. In July 1988, Iran agreed to the United Nations cease-fire, an act that Khomeini called "more deadly to me than drinking poison." At last the war that had seemed endless was over. Several hundred thousand men had died on each side. In the end, the border between the two countries remained where it had always been. The devastating war had changed nothing.

DESERT STORM

WHEN THE cease-fire was announced, the streets of Baghdad erupted in a spontaneous celebration of joy. Saddam Hussein presented the outcome as an Iraqi victory. In reality, though, the country was in a dismal state. Iraq owed $80 billion for the aid it had received from other countries during the war. It had an army of approximately 500,000 men, many of them without jobs to return to. Iraq's economy was in a shambles. But most disturbing to Saddam was the public mood. The Iraqi people, exhausted by nearly a decade of war and dictatorship, were restless. They expected that peace would bring not only prosperity but also greater freedom and more civil liberties—perhaps even democracy. Saddam could not permit these threats to his supremacy.

The Greek philosopher Plato wrote in the fourth century B.C., "When the tyrant has disposed of foreign enemies by conquest or treaty, and there is nothing to fear from them, then he is always stirring up some war or other, in order that the people may require a leader." The attention of the Iraqi people was drawn away from the failure of the war against Iran and their problems at home when Saddam began stirring up trouble with his neighbor to the southeast, Kuwait. He belligerently refused to repay his $10 billion war debt to Kuwait. He also returned to old grievances against Kuwait. He renewed his demand that Kuwait give Warba and Bubaiyan islands to Iraq so that Iraq could build a shipping port on the islands, and he repeated his accusation that Kuwait had stolen oil from Iraq's share of the Rumaila oilfield, which runs beneath their shared border. Once again he insisted that the border be redrawn.

Saddam signaled his intentions, but no one took him seriously. He proposed to Egypt's president, Hosni Mubarak, that they form an alliance to take over Saudi Arabia and Kuwait and share the spoils; Mubarak turned him down. Saddam made remarks to the kings of Jordan and Saudi Arabia about carving up Saudi territory and seizing Kuwait. The startled monarchs thought he was bluffing, or joking. Even when he massed troops near the Iraq-Kuwait border, no one believed he would really invade Kuwait. The leaders of the Gulf states, as well as the intelligence agencies of the United States and other Western nations, believed that Iraq did not have the resources to start a new war because its economy and its army had been weakened by the disastrous war against Iran. Representatives from Iraq and Kuwait met in Saudi Arabia to try to settle their countries' differences, but the negotiations broke down and each side accused the other of being unwilling to compromise. Iraq's negotiating team left Saudi Arabia on August 1, 1990.

The invasion of August 2 caught everyone nap-ping. Once again, however, just as when he had sent troops into Iran in 1980, Saddam Hussein had grossly misjudged the outcome of his action. He had expected to take Kuwait with no response from the rest of the world except a flurry of agitated hand-wringing. In-stead, he found himself facing formidable opposition from a broad coalition, or alliance, of nations, headed by the United States and including the industrialized European nations, the Soviet Union, Japan, and the other Persian Gulf states.

The United Nations Security Council quickly passed a resolution ordering Iraq to withdraw from Kuwait. Saddam ignored the UN, so the Security Council declared economic sanctions against Iraq. The United States and other nations had already frozen all Iraqi accounts in Western banks, preventing Iraq from withdrawing or doing business with funds held abroad. Now the UN sanctions banned all trade with Iraq. No goods could enter or leave the country. Iraq imported three-fourths of its food, and without imports the country would soon face shortages of bread and other basic goods. Unable to sell its oil abroad, it would soon be broke. Ships from the United States and other na-tions patrolled the Gulf to ensure that Iraqi tankers did not leave their ports. The UN hoped that the blockade would cripple Iraq's economy and force Saddam to withdraw from Kuwait.

Although the United States had supported Sad-dam against Iran, President George Bush promptly condemned him for the invasion of Kuwait. The Ameri-can response to the invasion was cloaked in layers of ambiguity. At first, Bush declared that the United States would not stand by and permit one nation's "naked aggression" toward another. But the United States had not intervened when China invaded Tibet in 1950, or when the Soviet Union invaded Afghanistan in 1979. Bush then said that the United States would take whatever action was needed to defend its allies in the Persian Gulf, despite the fact that the United States did not have a formal defense treaty with Kuwait, Saudi Arabia, or any other Gulf nation. Closer to the truth was Bush's statement that Saddam's invasion threatened America's "vital interests" in the Gulf. As everyone knew, Bush was talking about oil.

The Persian Gulf region contains nearly half the world's known oil reserves, and the United States depends heavily on imported Gulf oil. Bush's greatest fear was that Saddam would move on from Kuwait to invade Saudi Arabia. This would put Saddam in control of the largest concentration of oil reserves in the world. Although the president spoke about standing up to tyrants and defending the rule of law, Bush and many Americans also believed that the United States must protect one of the major sources of its energy.

The United States assembled an enormous multinational force in the deserts of Saudi Arabia. Although 30 countries sent troops and equipment, Americans made up the single largest group: 430,000 of them at the height of the troop buildup. At first, the coalition's purpose was to protect Saudi Arabia from invasion—to draw "a line in the sand" for Saddam to cross at his peril, said General Colin Powell, chairman of the Joint Chiefs of Staff and the nation's top military officer. The Americans called this defensive operation Desert Shield. Yet from the start, the coalition forces knew that they might be called upon to do more than defend Saudi Arabia. The United Nations set a deadline of

These Syrian soldiers driving a Soviet tank are part of the multi-national force assembled by the United States to push occupying Iraqi troops out of Kuwait.

January 15, 1991, for Iraq's peaceful withdrawal from Kuwait and approved the use of force if Saddam did not give in by that date.

As the weeks ticked off toward the deadline and the coalition force reached formidable proportions, Saddam tried several stalling tactics. Claiming that the conflict was between the United States and Iraq, he presented himself to other Arab nations as an Arab hero defending the Middle East against Western aggressors. He also tried to link his invasion of Kuwait with the Palestinian problem, saying that he would not withdraw until the United States and Israel agreed to a Palestinian state. Yasser Arafat of the Palestine Liberation Organization (PLO) and King Hussein of Jordan (no relation to Saddam Hussein) endorsed this position, which won Saddam a great deal of popular support in the Arab world. Bush and other coalition leaders, however, firmly rejected Saddam's attempt at "linkage" between the Palestine and Kuwait issues. Bush pointed out that the invasion of Kuwait had nothing at all to do with the plight of the Palestinians.

Another of Saddam's tactics involved foreign hostages. About 1.5 million foreigners, including 3,000 Americans, were living and working in Iraq and Kuwait at the time of the invasion. Saddam let most of the non-Western foreigners leave, and they streamed toward the Jordanian border. But he kept the Western diplomats, businesspeople, consultants, and teachers, many of whom were accompanied by their families, as hostages under armed guard. He threatened to use the hostages as "human shields," placing them at dams, military bases, and other sites that might be targeted by coalition missiles. The message to the Western powers was clear: If you attack me, your people will be the first to die. Most people outside Iraq were appalled by this cold-blooded use of civilians. They were further outraged when Saddam appeared on television visiting a group of the hostages, whom he called his "guests." Flanked by armed bodyguards, he smiled broadly as he patted a terrified young British boy named Stuart Lockwood on the head.

In the end, however, Saddam did not use his "human shield" plan. Instead, he released the hostages in December. Observers believe that he hoped a goodwill gesture might soften the coalition's resolve. Perhaps the antiwar voices in the United States would prevail, and he would be allowed to keep some or all of Kuwait without a fight. But despite heartfelt relief at the return of the hostages, the United Nations and the U.S.-led coalition stood firm.

The United States offered to negotiate a withdrawal strategy with Saddam right up until the deadline, but the Iraqi leader was evasive. Saddam Hussein found himself in a terrible predicament, like a bully who picks a fight with a weakling, only to discover that the weakling has a big, strong older brother. Saddam was facing a vastly superior force against which he could not win. Yet to back down would be to admit that he had made a mistake, to lose face in front of the Iraqi people and the world. Retreat might even mean his fall from power, for his enemies in Iraq would probably seize upon his failure in Kuwait as an excuse to overthrow him. He could not bring himself to take that chance. So he let events take their course, all the while trying desperately to present himself as the victim of Western imperialist aggression. Although Saddam's pose of injured righteousness was unconvincing to the outside world, his complete control of the media inside Iraq

Iraqi TV Taped Broadcast

Saddam Hussein horrified the world
when he appeared on television with
civilian hostages and smiled as he
patted a terrified boy on the head.

ensured that the Iraqi people saw their president in a heroic light, as the defender of Arab territory against a mighty Western attack.

On January 15, 1991, the deadline for withdrawal from Kuwait ran out. Two days later, Desert Shield became Desert Storm. The allied coalition shifted its purpose from defending Saudi Arabia to liberating Kuwait from Iraq. The coalition launched an air war, striking Iraqi military posts, communications centers, and missile launchers in both Kuwait and Iraq. Television viewers around the world watched as the night sky over Baghdad flared with rocket fire and the glow of burning buildings.

Saddam remained defiant, promising that the showdown with the U.S. forces would be "the mother of all battles" and that he would grind the Americans "into the mud and dust of defeat." He bombed the Israeli city of Tel Aviv, knowing that if Israel retaliated, other Arab countries might be drawn into the fray against Israel. But the United States was able to persuade Israel to remain out of the war, and sent antirocket missiles called Patriots to Israel to ward off further attack by Iraq's Scud rockets.

The Patriots and other high-tech weaponry gave the coalition a decided advantage over Saddam, particularly since most of the Iraqi air force had flown to Iran in the early days of the air war. It is still not clear whether the Iraqi pilots were defecting to their former enemy or whether Saddam made a deal with Iran to protect his aircraft from harm. At any rate, Iraq was technologically outmatched, although the Iraqis doggedly fought on. Troops and tanks on the ground took a terrible beating from the air assault.

February 20, 1991: Iraqis look at the rubble from buildings bombed by allied air raids on Baghdad during the Gulf War.

The second phase of the war began in February, when coalition ground troops surged into Iraq and Kuwait. In a well-planned move, coalition leader General Norman Schwarzkopf of the United States fooled Saddam into thinking that the coalition would attack on the Gulf coast. While Iraqi forces mobilized to meet the expected attack, coalition troops and tanks hurried through the desert to surround the bulk of the Iraqi army, cutting it off from retreat. The Iraqis surrendered by the hundreds, telling doleful tales of starvation in Iraq's ranks and of officers who had to force their reluctant men to fight at gunpoint. In less than four days of fighting on the ground, the allies took as many as 85,000 Iraqi prisoners of war, most of whom were thrilled to be fed, warm, and out of the fighting.

The ground war lasted only about 100 hours. Deploying the largest land force to be mobilized since World War II, the coalition swept the Iraqi occupying force out of Kuwait City and back across Iraq's border. Many Americans wondered: Why stop there? They thought that the United States ought to "finish the job" and destroy Saddam Hussein. Even Schwarzkopf showed some reluctance to halt the American advance. But Bush made it quite clear that the coalition's mission was to liberate Kuwait, not to seize Iraq or bring down Saddam. Many political analysts, however, suggest that Bush did not think it was necessary for U.S. forces to overthrow Saddam; he expected the frustrated and oppressed Iraqi people to do so.

Hopelessly outclassed on the battlefield and fighting to protect his own capital, Saddam Hussein agreed to the United Nations cease-fire on February 28. The Persian Gulf War was over. Casualties on the coalition side totaled 149 killed and 513 wounded. Iraq's casualty figures are not known, but experts estimate that 150,000 were killed. Peace activists in the United States and elsewhere say that this appalling death toll might have been avoided if the coalition had given the economic sanctions more time to work before resorting to force. On the other hand, Amnesty International's account of the atrocities performed against Kuwaitis by the occupying Iraqi troops suggests that the suffering in Kuwait would have been even greater had the occupation continued. As in every war, soldiers and ordinary people paid with their lives for the decisions of their leaders.

DOWN, BUT NOT OUT

DEFEATED IN WAR, Saddam Hussein resorted to vandalism on a colossal scale. Not only did the Iraqi occupying forces loot and trash hundreds of Kuwaiti homes and businesses, but before they withdrew they deliberately created the worst environmental disaster in history. They dynamited 800 of Kuwait's oil wells, 600 of which were set on fire, turning the midday sky black with smoke. They also blew up dozens of oil pipelines, tanks, and loaded tankers, creating an oil spill of 6 to 8 million barrels. (By way of comparison, the 1989 *Exxon Valdez* oil spill dumped 250,000 barrels of oil into Alaska's Prince William Sound.)

The fires and smoke dumped tons of soot, as well as hazardous chemicals such as carbon dioxide and sulfur dioxide, on Kuwait, Saudi Arabia, and Iraq. And although all fires were extinguished and all leaking wells were capped by November 1991—thanks to the efforts of an international crew of oil-fire experts—large areas of fragile desert and agricultural terrain had been dam-

In the aftermath of the Gulf War,
retreating Iraqi troops blew up
most of Kuwait's 950 oil wells—
gestures of defiance that darkened
the skies with soot and unleashed
dangerous pollutants into the air.

aged. In addition, scientists believe that among the long-term effects of the air pollution will be increased respiratory disease and acid rain in the Middle East.

The reefs, coastlines, and undersea ecosystems of the Persian Gulf were widely damaged by the oil slick. Some of the spilled oil belonged to Iraq, not Kuwait, a fact that emphasizes the meaninglessness and spitefulness of the destruction. Yet conservationists hope that the shock of Saddam's ecological sabotage has made the Gulf nations more aware of the need for environmental protection. In the wake of the disaster, Saudi Arabia and other countries set up marine parks and sanctuaries in critical Gulf habitats.

And what of Saddam Hussein? The aftermath of the Persian Gulf War illustrated once again the Iraqi president's remarkable ability to survive setbacks and to twist the truth. A few years earlier, he had declared that the UN cease-fire with Iran was really an Iraqi victory. Now he called for celebrations in Baghdad. "Iraq is the one that is victorious," he preposterously declared. "Iraq has punched a hole in the myth of American superiority and rubbed the nose of the United States in the dust. . . . We are confident that President Bush would never have accepted a cease-fire had he not been informed by his military leaders of the need to preserve the forces fleeing the fist of the heroic men of the Republican Guards."[1]

Saddam's claim of victory was applauded by many Iraqis, as well as by others in the Arab world, especially in Jordan and Egypt, where Iraq had had a strong measure of popular support during the Gulf War. They saw Saddam as a symbol of Arab pride and heroism for having stood up to the Western powers, even though Iraq was forced to retreat from Kuwait in the end. He proved that an Arab nation could be a major force in international affairs. To Saddam's admirers, the immense size and strength of the coalition force was evidence of Saddam's power: The allies had been forced to use all their might to combat him.

"Victory is not how many tanks or planes we or the enemy used," a Baath party newspaper announced. "Victory is the face that you acquire in the history books."[2] Saddam Hussein and his followers set about writing new history books to portray Hussein and Iraq as victors in the Gulf War. He had done the same thing before, on a much smaller scale, when he made a movie falsely glorifying his failed attempt to assassinate Qassim. He emerged from the assassination attempt a hero. But surviving the fiasco of defeat and humiliation in Kuwait was not easy for Saddam.

The end of the war brought precisely the domestic turmoil that Saddam had feared. Anti-Baath groups renewed their attacks on Saddam's regime, hoping to catch him at a weak moment. In the south, Shiite rebels—many of them supported by Iran—rose up against the army, making guerrilla attacks on military sites and calling for the population to overthrow Saddam. Kurdish rebels did the same thing in the north. Unfortunately for the insurrectionists, their plans misfired. The uprisings gave Saddam just the excuse he needed to rally the demoralized army against a new enemy.

Saddam saw the Kurds as the greater threat, so he launched a strong attack on the Kurdish region. As many as two million Kurds, dreading a repetition of earlier massacres and atrocities, fled across the borders into the desolate mountain hinterlands of Turkey and Iran. There, in the deepening winter of 1991–1992,

On the first anniversary of the Gulf War, Iraqis chant anti-American slogans while holding posters of the man they perceive to be a hero: Saddam Hussein.

they huddled in refugee camps. The United States, Great Britain, and France led an international effort to provide the Kurdish refugees with food and other emergency supplies and also to protect them from the Iraqi army. The allied task force eventually built a number of refugee camps inside Iraq's borders and declared that Iraqi planes could no longer fly over Iraqi territory north of the 36th parallel of latitude. This "no-fly" zone was intended to be a safe haven where the Kurds would be free from bombing raids, although no long-term solution to the problem was devised. The allies continued to enforce the no-fly zone and many Kurds returned to Iraq, but armed skirmishes and terrorism plagued relations between the Kurds and the country's Arab majority. The Kurds still hoped for an independent Kurdish state, but Saddam declared that he would not give up any territory to such a state. Iran and Turkey, too, refused to yield territory for a Kurdish homeland. The future of the Kurds looked bleak.

Although the Shiite uprising in the south received less international attention than the Kurdish insurrection, it was just as brutally crushed by Saddam's forces. As in the north, the allied task force imposed a no-fly zone over southern Iraq; this was intended to prevent Saddam from bombing Shiite resistance centers. But as with the Kurds, there seemed to be little hope of a permanent peace between the Iraqi government and the Shiite rebels. About 10,000 Shiite rebels took refuge in the marshes along the southern stretch of the Shatt-al-Arab. For centuries those marshes had served as the hiding place for outcasts and outlaws. They were also the traditional home of a people called the Marsh Arabs, who made their living by fishing in the maze of waterways; the Marsh Arabs numbered about 200,000 in the early 1990s. Saddam instructed the Iraqi army to build a series of dams and canals to drain the marshes. Although he claimed that his goal was to produce new agricultural land, the Shiites retorted that his only goal was to drive them out of their hiding places. In 1993 the army stepped up its attack on the marshes, using tanks and artillery guns. Troops poisoned the water and also set fires to make newly drained marshland uninhabitable. It appeared likely that Saddam would succeed in wiping out the remnants of Shiite resistance—and also the Marsh Arabs' livelihood.

Rumors and intelligence reports from Iraq said that in the confusing months following the Gulf War, Saddam was the target of several assassination attempts by disgruntled Iraqis. In March 1993, a London newspaper reported details of an Israeli plot to kill Saddam; the assassination was called off after some members of the assassination team were killed in a training accident. In the following month, Bill Clinton, the newly elected president of the United States, revealed that his country—barred by Congress from directly trying to kill a foreign leader—was spending millions of dollars each year on undercover programs aimed at toppling Saddam from power.

According to rumors that reached Western journalists, a plot against Saddam was discovered in July 1993. An Iraqi dissident declared that 500 or 600 army officers were accused of being involved in the coup plot and executed, but the Iraqi government never acknowledged this report. An official report was released, however, when another assassination attempt occurred in September 1993. As the presidential motorcade passed through the outskirts of Baghdad, a bomb exploded, wounding one of Saddam's bodyguards. Saddam's response was swift and severe. Sixty officials of the army, police, and government, including some members of Saddam's own Tikriti clan, were arrested; rumors said that as many as twenty were executed.

None of these efforts to loosen Saddam Hussein's grip on Iraq succeeded. Three years after the Persian Gulf War, Saddam was still in control. He had used several tactics to recover from the disasters of the Iran and Kuwait campaigns. He lavishly rewarded high-ranking officers in the armed forces and the secret police for their loyalty, and he increased the number of spies and informers to root out any potential disloyalty. He also carried out a massive propaganda war, with newspapers, murals, and speeches that proclaimed him an Islamic hero, a victor in war, and a father to the Iraqi people. As war damage in Baghdad was repaired, Saddam's image loomed larger than ever on billboards and walls. Whole museums were devoted to portraits of Saddam; schoolchildren spent hours drawing pictures of him. All of this hero worship was designed to reinforce the idea that Saddam was Iraq's savior.

Yet while the military and the secret police were wooed with pay raises and privileges, the ordinary people of Iraq were suffering shortages of food, medicine, consumer goods, and cash. But Saddam cleverly turned even his people's suffering into a propaganda tool. He claimed that the shortages were due to the United Nations economic sanctions, which were to remain in place until Iraq lived up to the agreements it had made at the time of the cease-fire—notably, to allow UN inspectors to examine all of Iraq's weapons factories and military bases for nuclear and chemical weapons. What Saddam did not tell the Iraqi people was that the UN sanctions did not apply to humanitarian supplies such as food and medicine, and that the UN offered to let Saddam sell $1.6 billion worth of oil to pay for such supplies. Saddam refused, saying that he would not let the UN tell him how to dispose of Iraq's oil. The Iraqi people, who were denied access to foreign newspapers, blamed the United Nations and the United States for hardships that were really caused by their own president.

Saddam steadfastly refused to comply with all of the United Nations resolutions that governed the 1991 cease-fire. He denied UN inspectors access to munitions factories, he violated the no-fly zones established to protect minorities within Iraq, and he threatened to shoot down planes carrying UN teams in Iraqi air space. His strategy was to stall and evade, all the while chipping away at the terms of the cease-fire, hoping to provoke a strong reaction from the West so that he would look like a victim of Western aggression. Twice there were air assaults against Iraq: In January 1993 the United States, Britain, and France bombed a number of military sites to enforce compliance with the UN resolutions, and in July 1993 the United States carried out a smaller raid after discovering evidence that Iraq had plotted to assassinate former president George Bush. These attacks did not cause much damage in Iraq; rather, they were intended as warnings to Saddam Hussein. But he did not appear ready to heed such warnings. After the July 1993 raid, Saddam declared that Iraq's confrontation with the United States would last a long time. And in the fall of 1993 he ordered several attacks on Kuwaiti border posts, causing some Kuwaitis to fear that he might be planning to send Iraqi troops across their borders a second time.

The Western press, drawing on Saddam's history of cruelty, brutality, arrogance, and unpredictability, sometimes portrayed him as a madman. But although he made errors in judgment, Saddam Hussein was far from irrational. Instead, he was a cold, calculating thinker. Every move he made in his career was aimed at one goal—getting power and keeping it. His success at gaining Western support during the Iran-Iraq war showed considerable skill at diplomatic manipulation. His ability to turn defeats into propaganda victories demonstrated a high degree of cunning and a shrewd knowledge of mob psychology. Yet it would be a mistake to dismiss his popularity in the Arab world as artificial, something sustained only by propaganda. Many Arabs, particularly the poor and dispossessed, admired Saddam because he had dared to defy the powerful Western nations. To those who hated and feared the United States and its allies, he was seen as a folk hero.

Above all, Saddam Hussein was a survivor. He survived grinding poverty and abuse as a child, prison, numerous assassination attempts and rebellions, and two punishing wars. Even after his defeat in the Persian Gulf War, said experts in Middle Eastern affairs, he could not be trusted to remain quietly within Iraq's borders. For a few days in late 1994, it looked as though they were right. On October 7, Saddam Hussein deployed 70,000 Iraqi troops, including two brigades of Republican Guards, just 12 miles (19 kilometers) from the Kuwait border. Iraqi sources announced that the troop movements were routine training maneuvers. Said the Iraqi News Agency, "Peace-loving Iraq has no aggressive intentions." To many in Kuwait and elsewhere, however, the troop buildup was an ominous reminder of the events just before the invasion of Kuwait.

President Bill Clinton ordered U.S. troops, warplanes, and ships to the Gulf to reinforce the several thousand U.S. marines already there. Britain, too, sent planes and soldiers. They wanted to let Saddam Hussein know that any attempt to cross Kuwait's border would bring a swift, harsh response. Within a week, the Iraqi troops were withdrawing from the border, and a few days later Iraq opened several top-secret military sites to UN observers. The threat of war had receded. But the incident provoked disagreements among the members of the United Nations Security Council. Russia and France favored a conciliatory approach to Iraq, suggesting that the UN should end the embargo that had kept Iraq from selling its oil—and kept everything but food and humanitarian necessities from entering Iraq—since the end of the Gulf War. The United States and Britain, however, insisted that first Saddam would have to meet two crucial conditions: He would have to formally acknowledge that Kuwait was an independent, sovereign state, and he would have to agree to long-term monitoring by the UN of Iraq's weapons programs.

The events of October 1994 proved one thing: Despite growing frustration among the Iraqi people and fierce rebellion by the Shiites and the Kurds, Hussein was still firmly in control of his country. In light of his relentless struggle to stay in power, most observers felt it unlikely that Saddam Hussein would ever willingly step down from the presidency of Iraq. His rise to power had been accomplished by violence; many in Iraq and around the world wondered whether he would fall the same way.

CHRONOLOGY

3200 B.C.   Sumerian civilization reaches its height in Meso-
            potamia.

600   Babylon is rebuilt by King Nebuchadnezzar.

539   Babylon falls to the Persians.

637 A.D.   Arabs conquer Mesopotamia and introduce the Is-
            lamic faith.

1534   The Ottoman empire, based in Turkey, gains con-
            trol of Iraq.

1899   The sheikhdom of Kuwait comes under British
            protection.

1914–18   The Ottoman empire collapses during World
            War I.

1920   Britain creates the modern nation of Iraq from
            three Ottoman provinces.

1921	Iraq becomes a kingdom under King Faisal I but continues to be administered by Britain.
1932	Iraq becomes independent.
1937	Saddam Hussein is born near Tikrit on April 28.
1957	Saddam Hussein joins the Baath party.
1958	General Abdul Karim Qassim overturns the Iraqi monarchy in a coup.
1959	Saddam Hussein and other Baathists try to assassinate Qassim; Saddam Hussein is injured.
1961	Kuwait becomes an independent nation.
1963	The Baathists seize control of Iraq in a coup. Nine months later, the Baathists are overthrown in turn.
1964	Saddam Hussein founds the secret police branch of the Baath party. In October he is arrested by the military government.
1966	Saddam escapes from jail in Baghdad.
1968	The Baathists again take over Iraq. Saddam Hussein is the number two leader in the new government.
1979	The Ayatollah Ruhollah Khomeini rises to power in Iran. Saddam Hussein becomes president of Iraq.
1980	Iraq invades Iran, starting war between the two nations.
1988	Iraq and Iran declare a cease-fire. Iraq uses chemical weapons against the Kurds of northern Iraq.

1990   Iraq invades Kuwait. Saddam Hussein declares that Kuwait is a province of Iraq.

1991   The United States and its allies drive Iraq out of Kuwait in the Persian Gulf War. Before leaving Kuwait, Iraqi forces create an environmental disaster. Iraq again attacks its Kurdish population.

1993   The United States launches missiles against an Iraqi military post after learning of a plot to assassinate former president George Bush.

1994   In October Iraq deploys 70,000 troops near the Kuwait border, then withdraws them when the U.S. and allies begin sending troops, warplanes, and ships to the Gulf.

NOTES

CHAPTER ONE
OVERNIGHT INVASION

1. Judith Miller and Laurie Mylroie, *Saddam Hussein and the Crisis in the Gulf,* New York: Random House/Times Books, 1990, p. 212.

2. Paul Gray, "The Man Behind the Demonic Image," *Time,* February 11, 1991, p. 36.

CHAPTER TWO
THE BIRTHPLACE OF HISTORY

1. Adel Darwish and Gregory Alexander, *Unholy Babylon: The Secret History of Saddam's War,* New York: St. Martin's Press, 1991, p. 198.

2. Judith Miller and Laurie Mylroie, *Saddam Hussein and the Crisis in the Gulf,* New York: Random House/Times Books, 1990, p. 65.

3. Miller and Mylroie, p. 70.

CHAPTER THREE
COMING-OF-AGE IN BAGHDAD

1. Efraim Karsh and Inauri Rautsi, *Saddam Hussein: A Political Biography*, New York: Free Press, 1991, p. 166.

2. Karsh and Rautsi, p. 15.

3. Judith Miller and Laurie Mylroie, *Saddam Hussein and the Crisis in the Gulf*, New York: Random House/Times Books, 1991, pp. 37–38.

4. Quoted in Miller and Mylroie, p. 30.

5. Adel Darwish and Gregory Alexander, *Unholy Babylon: The Secret History of Saddam's War*, New York: St. Martin's Press, 1991, p. 197.

CHAPTER FOUR
THE MASTER OF TERROR

1. Samir al-Khalil, *Republic of Fear: The Politics of Modern Iraq*, Berkeley and Los Angeles: University of California Press, 1989, p. 59.

2. Adel Darwish and Gregory Alexander, *Unholy Babylon: The Secret History of Saddam's War*, New York: St. Martin's Press, 1991, p. 201.

3. Judith Miller and Laurie Mylroie, *Saddam Hussein and the Crisis in the Gulf*, New York: Random House/Times Books, 1991, pp. 31–32.

4. Darwish and Alexander, p. 202.

5. Quoted in Efraim Karsh and Inauri Rautsi, *Saddam Hussein: A Political Biography*, New York: Free Press, 1991, p. 31.

CHAPTER FIVE
"LONG LIVE SADDAM!"

1. The Samira Shahbandar incident and Uday Hussein's murder of the servant are described in Efraim Karsh and Inauri

Rautsi, *Saddam Hussein: A Political Biography*, New York: Free Press, 1991, p. 184, and Judith Miller and Laurie Mylroie, *Saddam Hussein and the Crisis in the Gulf*, New York: Random House/Times Books, 1990, p. 39.

2. Samir al-Khalil, *Republic of Fear: The Politics of Modern Iraq*, Berkeley and Los Angeles: University of California Press, 1989, p. 52.

3. *Kurdish Affairs Bulletin*, quoted in Karsh and Rautsi, p. 71.

CHAPTER SIX
THE NEW NEBUCHADNEZZAR

1. Judith Miller and Laurie Mylroie, *Saddam Hussein and the Crisis in the Gulf.* New York: Random House/Times Books, 1990, p. 143.

2. *The New York Times*, April 3, 1984, quoted in Samir al-Khalil, *Republic of Fear: The Politics of Modern Iraq*, Berkeley and Los Angeles: University of California Press, 1989, p. 63.

3. Khalil, p. 78.

CHAPTER EIGHT
DOWN BUT NOT OUT

1. Efraim Karsh and Inauri Rautsi, *Saddam Hussein: A Political Biography*, New York: Free Press, 1991, p. 266.

2. Jerry Adler, "The Final Push," *Newsweek*, Spring/Summer 1991 Special Issue, p. 101.

BIBLIOGRAPHY

Begley, Sharon. "Saddam's Ecoterror: The Iraqi Oil Flood Creates Environmental Hazards and Military Obstacles." *Newsweek*, February 4, 1991, p. 36.

Bratman, Fred. *War in the Persian Gulf.* Brookfield, Conn.: The Millbrook Press, 1991.

Bullock, John, and Harvey Morris. *Saddam's War: The Origins of the Kuwait Conflict and the International Response.* London: Faber & Faber, 1991.

Canby, Thomas Y. "The Persian Gulf: After the Storm." *National Geographic*, August 1991, p. 2.

Chadwick, Frank. *Desert Shield Fact Book.* New York: Berkeley, 1991.

Darwish, Adel, and Gregory Alexander. *Unholy Babylon: The Secret History of Saddam's War.* New York: St. Martin's Press, 1991.

Duffy, Brian, and Richard Z. Chesnoff. "The Next Battle with Saddam." *U.S. News and World Report*, August 10, 1992, p. 20.

Foster, Leila M. *Iraq*. Chicago: Childrens Press, 1991.

Gray, Paul. "The Man Behind the Demonic Image," *Time*, February 11, 1991, p. 36.

Hawley, T. M. *Against the Fires of Hell*. New York: Harcourt Brace Jovanovich, 1992.

Karsh, Efraim, and Inauri Rautsi. *Saddam Hussein: A Political Biography*. New York: Free Press, 1991.

Khalil, Samir al-. "Iraq and Its Future." *The New York Times Review of Books*, April 11, 1991, p. 10.

————. *Republic of Fear: The Politics of Modern Iraq*. Berkeley and Los Angeles: University of California Press, 1989.

Lerner Department of Geography. *Iraq in Pictures*. Minneapolis: Lerner Publications, 1990.

Marr, Phebe. "Iraq's Uncertain Future." *Current History*, January 1991, p. 1.

————. *The Modern History of Iraq*. Boulder, Colo.: Westview Press, 1985.

McGrath, Peter, and colleagues. "More Than a Madman," *Newsweek*, January 7, 1991, p. 20.

Metz, Helen C. *Iraq: A Country Study*. Washington: United States Government Printing Office, 1990.

Miller, Judith, and Laurie Mylroie. *Saddam Hussein and the Crisis in the Gulf*. New York: Random House/Times Books, 1990.

Oppenheim, Leo. *Ancient Mesopotamia: Portrait of a Dead Civilization*. Chicago: University of Chicago Press, 1977.

Renfrew, Nita. *Saddam Hussein*. New York: Chelsea House, 1992.

Roux, Georges. *Ancient Iraq*. Harmondsworth, England: Penguin Books, 1980.

Sciolino, Elaine. *Outlaw State: Saddam's Quest for Power and the Gulf Crisis*. New York: Wiley, 1991.

Simon, Bob. *Forty Days*. New York: Putnam's, 1992.

Simon, Reeva S. *Iraq Between the Two World Wars: The Creation and Implementation of a Nationalist Ideology*. New York: Columbia University Press, 1986.

INDEX

Ibrahim, Hassan, 21–22
Ibrahim, Subha, 21, *23*
Illah, Abdul, 34
Iran, 29, 33, 65–68, 73, 76–78, 80, 81, 83, 84, 89, 90, 111
Islam, 26, 28–31, 59, 67, 76, 84
Israel, 26, 35, 55, 63, 67, 81, 83, 98, 108

Jews, 35, 70–71
Jihaz Haneen, 54, 56, 60, 71
Jordan, 55, 83, 91, 104

al-Kailani, Rashid Ali, 34–35
Karbala, 28
Karsh, Efraim, 38
Kazzar, Nadhim, 73
Kemp, Geoffrey, 84
Khomeini, Ayatollah Ruhollah, 68, *69*, 71, 76, 77, 79, 81, 83, 84, 89
Khuzistan, 77–79
Kirkuk oilfields, 72, 73
Kurds, 19, 32–33, 43, 72–73, 81, 83, 105, 107, 112
Kuwait, 11–12, *13*, 14–16, 18–19, 31, 33, 65, 66, 83, 89, 91–93, 95, 96, *97*, 98, 100–102, 112

League of Nations, 32, 34, 35
Lebanon, 32

al-Majid, Hussein Kamel, 60

al-Majid al-Tikriti, Hussein, 21
Marr, Phebe, 30
Marsh Arabs, 107–108
Mecca, 28
Mesopotamia, 24, 26, 28
Mongols, 30
Mosul, 30, 32, 45
Mubarak, Hosni, 16, 91
Muhammad, 26, 28, 77, 86
Mukhabarat, 15

Najaf, 28
Nasser, Gamal Abdel, 40–41, 45
Nationalism, 34, 65
Nazi Germany, 34, 35
Nebuchadnezzar, 107, 110
Nuclear weapons, 19, 81, 109

Oil, 63–66, 93, 102, *103*, 104, 110
Organization of Petroleum Exporting Countries (OPEC), 65–66
Osiraq power plant, 81, 83
Ottoman empire, 30–32

Palestine, 32, 35
Palestinian Arabs, 35, 63, 95
Pan-Arabism, 34, 42, 68
Persians, 26, 28
Plato, 90–91
Powell, Colin, 93
Purges, 68, 70–75

Qasr-al-Nihayyat, 51, 53–54